STO

ACPL ITEM
DISCARDED

ALLEN COUNTY PUBLIC LIBRARY
3 1833 00155 1925

Y0-ABY-404

*616.89
D71p

Dominian,Jacob   Hawthorn,1962

Psychiatry and the Christian

1195329,

9-16-58

NOV 13 '62

PSYCHIATRY AND THE
CHRISTIAN

IS VOLUME

93

OF THE

Twentieth Century Encyclopedia of Catholicism

UNDER SECTION

IX

THE CHURCH AND THE MODERN WORLD

IT IS ALSO THE

93RD

VOLUME IN ORDER OF PUBLICATION

Edited by **HENRI DANIEL-ROPS** *of the Académie Française*

PSYCHIATRY AND THE CHRISTIAN

By J. DOMINIAN

HAWTHORN BOOKS · PUBLISHERS · *New York*

Copyright © 1962 by Hawthorn Books, Inc., 70 Fifth Avenue, New York 11, N. Y. Copyright under International and Pan-American Copyright Conventions. Philippines Copyright 1962 by Hawthorn Books, Inc. All rights reserved, including the right to reproduce this book, or portions thereof, in any form, except for the inclusion of brief quotations in a review. This book was manufactured in the United States of America and published simultaneously in Canada by McClelland & Stewart, Ltd., 25 Hollinger Road, Toronto 16. The Library of Congress has catalogued The Twentieth Century Encyclopedia of Catholicism under card number 58-14327. Library of Congress Catalogue card number for this volume: 62-18500. The Catholic University of America Library has catalogued this volume based on the Lynn-Peterson Alternative Classification for Catholic Books: BQT184.T9v.93/RC455.D67. Suggested decimal classification for this book: 616.89.

First Edition, September, 1962

NIHIL OBSTAT

Daniel Duivesteijn, S.T.D.

Censor Deputatus

IMPRIMATUR

Georgius L. Craven

Vicarius Generalis

Westmonasterii, die XXIX MAII MCMLXII

The Nihil obstat and Imprimatur are a declaration that a book or pamphlet is considered to be free from doctrinal or moral error. It is not implied that those who have granted the Nihil obstat and Imprimatur agree with the contents, opinions, or statements expressed.

H-9521

1195329

CONTENTS

INTRODUCTION

Psychiatry as a specialized branch of medicine has been making steady advances throughout this century. Since the last war the progress has been greatly accelerated and we are now entering a phase when we can confidently expect to begin to master some of the illnesses that for long have baffled science. The subject by its very nature impinges considerably on adjacent disciplines of theology, metaphysics, sociology and philosophy. Some of these are territories which the Church has developed for 2000 years and she is a jealous guardian of the truths unfolded in the process. Controversies are bound to arise which, if conducted meaningfully, can prove of considerable mutual assistance to one side or the other. There has been, however, a tendency to concentrate on erudite issues on the fringe of the subject and to leave a good deal of the substance of clinical psychiatry out of the discussion. In this book an attempt has been made to familiarize readers with current concepts of psychiatric disorders and some of their implications for Christianity. It is inevitable, in the available space, that the presentation of some subjects has been curtailed. Emphasis has been deliberately placed on facts of psychiatric practice rather than on discussion of specialized issues. References are given to works of various authors which deal with particular subjects. The present urgent need is to acquaint all those, whose work brings them frequently in contact with these problems, with the basic essentials of psychiatry and Christianity. This knowledge should have an important bearing on the judgement which the Christian has to make on his own or his neighbour's difficulties. It is my sincere hope that it will prove of particular assistance to the pastoral clergy who have so often to bear the brunt of advising and guiding those in need of help.

I am much indebted to my teachers at the postgraduate Institute of Psychiatry for the psychiatric training and high standards which have made this book possible. In particular, my sincere thanks are due to Sir Aubrey Lewis, not only for his most helpful criticisms and suggestions, but also for his unyielding and continuous example to his students in seeking truth relentlessly whether in psychiatry or any other discipline worthy of human pursuit. My thanks are also due to Dr R. Hobson and Fr H. Keldany for their encouragement and advice. Finally, it is difficult to acknowledge sufficiently the debt I owe to my wife for her labours in the preparation of this book. Without her continuous support, it is doubtful whether the manuscript would have seen the light of day.

HISTORY OF PSYCHO-
LOGICAL MEDICINE

The history of all ancient civilizations contains references and descriptions of mental disorders. Chinese, Indian, Mexican, Egyptian and Mesopotamian accounts all show a fairly uniform concept of insanity as a visitation of spirits and deities, often as a punishment for some transgression of divine or ethical laws. Sin was equated not only with spiritual disorder but as precursor and cause of physical and psychological illness, a view still prevalent amongst primitive tribes. On this basis, cure was only possible by the placation of the offended power with the necessary rituals and the acknowledgment of sin, accompanied by suitable expiation.

The Greek era saw the transformation of medical practice from a mystical to a rational basis. The emphasis now shifted to disorder of the physis, or nature, and physiological medicine was conceived. Hippocrates (460–377 B.C.) has been called the Father of Medicine. He was a keen observer of natural phenomena and mental illnesses were carefully described. He recognized mania, melancholia, puerperal psychoses, deliria, phobic reactions and hysteria, explaining the latter condition on the basis of the wandering of the uterus throughout the body, hence the name of the condition. His most outspoken and historically famous remarks are concerned with the subject of epilepsy, the sacred disease. "It thus appears to me to be in no way more divine or more sacred than other diseases, but has a natural cause from which it originates like other affections.... If you cut open the head you will find the brain humid, full of sweat and smelling badly. And in this way you may see that it is not a god which injures the body but disease." Nearly 2500 years later, Professor Penfield[1] in Canada and others have done exactly what Hippocrates suggested, operated on the brain of epileptics, finding and removing the anticipated damaged areas, with resultant cures.

The revolutionary views of Hippocrates did not eradicate the traditional beliefs of the relationship between mental illness and religion. Neither Plato nor Aristotle supported this view. There was a gradual diminution of emphasis of the physical etiology and a corresponding rise of philosophical and religious explanations. This development, now linked with the devil, demons and demoniacal possession of the Christian era, had adverse effects on the management of these patients who were envisaged as instruments of the devil and thus became objects of fear and inevitably of retribution.

The ill-treatment of the mentally ill is a recurrent theme in the history of Western civilization of the last 2000 years. Already in the second century A.D. Soranus introduced humanitarian methods; Caelius Aurelianus, in the fourth century, attacks the use of chains and flogging and advises the minimum use of physical restraint and others, both lay and professional, down to our own times, are to be found repeatedly trying to stem and reverse the rising tides of cruelty and indifference.

The early period of the Middle Ages saw the rise of Arabian medicine. Rhazes (841–926), Avicenna (980–1037) are names of great physicians interested in psychiatric illness, moderate and humane in their treatment and responsible for the development of hospitals for the sick in mind.

[1] W. Penfield and K. Paine, "Results of Surgical Therapy for Focal Epileptic Seizures", *Canadian Medical Association Journal* (1955), LXXIII, p. 515.

By the beginning of the thirteenth century, scientific interest in the subject virtually came to an end and for the next few hundred years Europe became the centre of a gathering storm with profound religious, social and political upheaval. In these disturbed centuries, when the security and the certainty of an established order were reduced to fragments, when society and individuals needed props and scapegoats, the mentally ill were an easy prey. While the Black Death spread havoc, we see mass hysterical phenomena in the dancing manias and a mixture of hysteria and masochism in the flagellant processions. But the most potent and ultimately most destructive weapon was the emergence of witch hunting.

Two Dominican friars, Julius Sprenger and Heinrich Kramer, with unrivalled zeal, set about the task of proving the existence of witches, their possession by the devil and the need for one treatment only, torture and burning. They collected their information and proposed their thesis in the infamous *Malleus Maleficarum*, the Witches' Hammer, published towards the end of the fifteenth century. "This then is our proposition, devils by their art do bring about evil effects through witchcraft." After asserting the greater number of women witches and the wickedness of woman, they conclude: "All witchcraft comes from carnal lust which is in women insatiable. . . . Wherefore for the sake of fulfilling their lusts they consort with devils." There are detailed descriptions of the marks of witchcraft, now familiar symptoms and signs of hysteria, schizophrenia and other mental conditions. Having received the approval of the emperor, the University of Cologne and a papal Bull, they proceeded to put their beliefs into practice. Thousands of victims, a great proportion of whom were women, were burned at the stake. Undoubtedly the majority were mentally sick. The work of Sprenger and Kramer in no way diminished with the Reformation, whose leaders continued this execrable persecution. The last witch was burned in 1782 in Switzerland.

In the midst of these tragic events not everyone was silent. Johann Weyer (1515–88), an extremely competent physician who took unusual interest in mental illness and has been called the "true founder" of modern psychiatry, studied the problem of witches in minute detail and presented his findings in the *De Praestigiis Dæmonum*. He came to the conclusion that witches were sick people and in need of treatment. Remaining a devout and practising Catholic, he could not agree with the current outlook and succinctly expressed his views: "It is highly unpleasant to see how people, in order to kill errors, are busy killing human beings"— a lesson which humanity has yet to learn. Juan Luis Vives (1492–1540) was a Spaniard, an exceedingly devout man with a wide range of interests, a penetrating intellect and a gentle disposition, immensely interested in improving the state of all those in need, including the sick in mind. He defended the status of women and wrote of their nobility at a time when they were being subjected to the vilifications of the witch-hunters. He urged humane treatment for the inmates of asylums and deprecated unnecessary force or restraint. His empirical observations on some psychological issues have earned for him the title of the Father of modern empirical psychology. He dismissed the influence of the planets on mental functioning, and studied the rôle of the emotions in memory processes. Reginald Scot, an Englishman and like Vives a layman, who published in 1584 *The Discoverie of Witchcraft*, came to the same conclusions about witchcraft and disease and wondered how people could be so deceived. The deception continued, however, and James I ordered Scot's book to be burned.

Also, during these centuries, hospitals for the mentally ill were built in various parts of Europe. One of the most famous was the Bethlem Hospital in London, one of the oldest hospitals in Europe continuously receiving the mentally ill since its inception. The standard of care varied enormously, however, and often conditions were lamentable.

The seventeenth and eighteenth centuries produced a number of eminent philosophers, Descartes, Hobbes, Spinoza,

Leibniz, Locke, Berkeley, Butler, Hume and Hartley. They developed ideas on knowledge, perception, the unconscious and mind-body relationships which have had a profound influence on modern psychiatric issues.

While these thinkers discussed these concepts, the plight of mental patients continued to be unsatisfactory in the treatment they received. Treatment is an euphemistic term, for if the zeal for burning abated, the well nigh universal policy of social isolation, restraint and roughness held little hope for recovery.

These methods were now assiduously attacked by two great reformers, the French doctor Philippe Pinel (1745–1826) and the Quaker merchant, William Tuke (1732–1822). Pinel obtained his medical degree in 1773 in the University of Toulouse. He was appointed head of the Bicêtre, a big asylum, in 1793 and after first convincing the revolutionary tribunals set about his work of reform. "The mentally ill, far from being guilty persons who merit punishment, are sick people whose miserable state deserves all the consideration due to suffering humanity." Inspired by such views, he set about freeing the patients from their chains, stopped cruel and useless treatments such as bloodletting and cold baths and fostered a personal interest for the individual patients, encouraging useful occupations throughout the day and a sympathetic hearing of their troubles. He visited the sick daily, made notes on their progress and was not afraid to discharge those he thought able to cope with life.

The death of a friend of William Tuke in an asylum drew his attention to the appalling conditions existing in these institutions and, with the help of the Society of Friends, he set up the Retreat in York in 1796. There the approach was similar to the methods of Pinel. In the United States, Dorothea Lynde Dix, a New England school teacher, took up a similar fight on behalf of the mentally ill and, over a number of years, was responsible for the building of many mental hospitals and the establishment of reasonable standards of care and treatment. In the efforts of Tuke and Dix, we see the active rôle of the layman in an area where psychiatry was lagging lamentably behind in its share of fundamental advances made in adjacent spheres of medicine. The only weapons available were kindness, careful attention to food, hygiene, the elimination of cruelty in the name of therapy, and the stimulation of interest in useful occupations and suitable activities. This approach came to be known as moral treatment which remained the standard approach until recent decades which have seen significant breakthroughs in treatment.

By the middle of the nineteenth century, psychological medicine was beginning to become better organized, special clinics were being set up in university centres and eminent men were emerging, especially in France and Germany. Two names stand out. The first is that of Emil Kraepelin (1856–1926), a German psychiatrist who brought order to a descriptive chaos and who was able to classify patterns of disease such as dementia praecox, the precursor of schizophrenia and the manic depressive illnesses. Although modified and improved subsequently by others, especially the Swiss psychiatrist Eugene Bleuler (1857–1939) who introduced the word schizophrenia, these classifications have stood the test of time. While interest was thus concentrated on these severe forms of illnesses, the psychoses, Sigmund Freud (1856–1939), who spent most of his life in Vienna, concentrated on the neuroses. With singular single-mindedness, in the face of much criticism, he illuminated brilliantly a field of disturbances which hitherto had been imprisoned in the physical "causes". In a series of studies, publication of which began in 1895, he indicated the rôle of the emotions, of the unconscious and of the early years of childhood in the etiology of neurotic illness. He described psychopathological mechanisms which have since become everyday notions in psychiatric practice and he has left behind a vast number of theories which are controversial issues to this very day. There is very little doubt that he and the other great figures of the psychoanalytical school have added a new dimension in psychological thought both in terms of theories expounded and the closely linked revolution in treatment by psychotherapeutic methods.

Freud's work brings us right up to the fourth decade of our present century. Even before his death his efforts to treat neurotic illness by psychotherapy were beginning to be matched by physical methods of treatment such as electro-convulsive therapy for depressive illnesses, insulin shock therapy for schizophrenia and prefrontal leucotomy for a variety of disorders. In the last decade, a new range of drugs, the tranquillizers and antidepressants, have added richly to the range of treatment and success for the vast army of sufferers. The last group of drugs is the fruit of extensive research in the biochemistry of psychiatric illness and it can be confidently expected that further successes will crown such efforts. Side by side with this work, psychiatrists, penologists and sociologists have been studying a series of matters with relevant issues for them all. Adult crime, juvenile delinquency, the social conditions which give rise to crime or illness are subjects which can profit by a combined approach, the contributory physical, psychological and social factors coming under careful scrutiny, and, wherever possible, receiving the appropriate remedy.

Above all, the status of psychiatric illness and of its sufferers is undergoing a radical transformation. The social stigma of these conditions is receding and they are being gradually incorporated in the accepted range of illnesses. Treatment in hospital has gradually become a less formal affair and the Mental Health Act of 1959 has crystallized these movements in Great Britain by removing the special designation of mental hospitals, making every hospital fit to receive and treat psychological disturbances on a basis which, for the patient, is indistinguishable from those receiving treatment for any other illness.

CHAPTER II

FOUNDATIONS OF
PERSONALITY

Traditional Christian views hold that man, God's creation, is a unity of soul and body, endowed with a rational free will, capable of choosing or rejecting God and destined to share his presence for eternity. After the original sin of Adam and Eve, he forfeited his right to the sonship of God, but was redeemed in the fullness of time by Christ, the Son of God. But if this relationship was thus restored and the freedom of the will retained, the integrity of his nature was not. His passage through this vale of tears is saddled with an unruly and disordered nature continually in need of God's grace to strengthen and sustain it towards its ultimate goal. While the sacraments, prayer and good deeds are the means of enrichment of grace, the latter acts upon and operates through this unity of body and soul. The nature and function of the soul is the domain of theology in so far as revelation and faith are involved. As soul itself, the nature and function of the soul is the proper domain of both philosophy and psychology, whether rational or clinical. In this connection, of equal importance is the ever-growing knowledge of the physical and psychological part of man and the contribution of psychology is the subject of this chapter. Without entering into the long-standing controversies about soma, soul and psyche, it is nevertheless abundantly clear that, while these entities are independent, there is need for their healthy functioning and harmonious interdependence. Faith, tradition and the living authority of the Church provide an evolving but consistent and stable framework for the life of the spirit. The foundations and growth of the human personality have no such definite equivalents and exist precariously between an ever-growing ring of rival claims. What follows is a short introduction to the main theories currently contributing to our knowledge of the springs and development of the human personality.

PSYCHOANALYTIC THEORIES

There is little doubt that in this arena the figure of Freud casts its long and imperative shadow. The man who, with the minimum of sophistication, pronounced religion to be the universal neurosis, declared God to be a fictitious projection and denied the freedom of the will, is understandably a scientist with creeds totally unacceptable to Christianity. This, coupled with his overwhelming emphasis on sexuality as the driving impulse of human conduct, produced a spontaneous revulsion against both his theories and the associated treatment techniques which have been suspected of doing little more than spread immorality through a smoke screen of professional respectability. These reactions, while understandable, are only partially justified. It is widely acknowledged that Freud, with no formal training in philosophy or theology, has minimal claims to authority in either and his pronouncements in these fields are proportionately insignificant. His claim to greatness, which I consider undeniable, is his energetic development of the rôle of the unconscious and the emotions in human behaviour and the construction of an architectural design of thought and theory which has revolutionized psychiatric concepts.

Freud had made his mark both in pharmacology and neurology before he turned his attention to the treatment of neurotic patients. He was soon dissatisfied with the then available treatments and concentrated his attention on allowing his patients to talk about themselves, their symptoms and past incidents. It became apparent that some of these experiences, long forgotten, had painful emotional overtones which had materially contributed to the presenting symptoms of the patient. By his passing no judgement of any kind, patients were encouraged to recall and relive verbally these episodes, which frequently happened to be sexual incidents, real or imaginary. This recounting, or abreaction, proved highly efficacious and soon led Freud to formulate the view that such unpleasant traumatic events, taking place almost always in childhood, although removed from consciousness, had nevertheless actively persisted in the unconscious. The unconscious was one of the central themes of Freud's work. Without placing it in any identifiable part of man, he studied its intrinsic operations by means of dreams, slips of the tongue, unintentional and mistaken acts; he went on to demonstrate that there is this part of man's psyche, which, although by definition totally unknown, exerts an effective influence on everyday behaviour and phantasy life. He then went on to postulate his other major hypotheses, namely that the two main driving energies, apart from self-preservation, were the instinct of sex, given the special title of libido, and later on, with much less elaboration, he added the second, an innate tendency towards self-destruction. Freud was considerably attracted by the duality of qualities and here was a neat apposition of Eros and Thanatos, the names he attached to mankind's supreme ends.

The concept of libido was extended to cover much more than adult sexual experiences; it came to convey a pool of energy derived from all sources of pleasurable experiences, bodily, aesthetic and those arising from interpersonal relations. The development, use and misuse of libido were the foundations for his theory of personality and psychiatric disorder.

In the growth of the young child, there are described three vital periods of sexual development, the oral, anal and phallic stages. The mouth provides the first pleasurable transaction for the young infant with breast or bottle feeding and later on weaning. At about the end of the first year, attention is diverted to elimination with emphasis laid on cleanliness and orderliness. For the first time the child is faced with confused and incomprehensible requests as the adult's revulsion to the excretory function and the mother's anxiety to achieve speedily an accepted routine are communicated to him. What is a natural and pleasurable experience is now surrounded with alternating responses of approval and opprobrium and the lifelong mechanism of suppressing immediate satisfaction to gain approval or avoid punishment, the mother's in this context, is initiated. At about three, there is the third shift of emphasis and now the child concentrates his attention on the genitals, evaluating the differences between the sexes and deriving such satisfaction as accidental or deliberate manipulation may invoke. Needless to say that such activities are entirely free of any moral responsibility on the part of the child. The conclusion of this stage is reached with the Oedipus complex, an attraction of the child for the parent of the opposite sex, with a simultaneous opposition and hostility for the father in the case of the boy, and for the mother in the case of the girl, who are regarded as rivals. This attraction, mainly unconscious, is repressed and the resolution of the complex is found in the adoption of the characteristics of femininity for the girl and masculinity for the boy; in technical terms identifying with the parent of the same sex. From about seven to twelve, there is, sexually speaking, a latent period with attention diverted to the development of the social and cultural ethos of the community. Finally, the advent of puberty is initiated by complicated physical and hormonal changes, establishing the pattern of adult sexual tendencies.

As indicated, the smooth and satisfactory completion of each phase is considered of vital importance. Conflicts, undue prolongation, unsatisfactory relations of the nursing couple with excessive submission on the part of the child, inculcation of undue fear about sexual matters by the parents, are visualized as fixing an excessive libido at that particular stage, the source of later neurotic disorder, sexual perversions and permanent changes in the personality. Thus excessive passivity or aggression may ensue from the oral stage, while traits of obstinacy, pedantic attention to detail, undue concern with cleanliness and order, uncertainty with the need to check and recheck, right through to the highly complex rituals of obsessional illness are related to disturbance of the anal stages.

Side by side with this theory of personality, Freud developed a model for its structural organization. There are three constituents, the id, composed mainly of those instinctual drives, urges and desires entirely unconscious but striving for expression. The superego is the second component, mainly unconscious, incorporating all the environmental prohibitions, particularly parental, which surround the person through development. This is seen as a severe taskmaster, imposing excessive demands and exacting retribution, making its presence known after some apparently neutral conduct, which contravenes its dictates, with an overwhelming feeling of guilt which, since unconscious, remains unexplainable to the person experiencing it. The difference between this excessive, incomprehensible, unrelated and apparently unprovoked sense of guilt and ordinary guilt, experienced after a conscious infringement of the natural and moral law, is of vital importance. The former presents a pathological entity, immune to the healing procedure of contrition and reparation and usually in need of psychiatric intervention, the latter is an everyday issue amenable to ordinary spiritual help. The ego, which completes the triad, is the conscious, rational component of man, in continuous contact with the inner and outer environment, applying ordinary values and judgement, and is the part of man from which conscience as ordinarily understood operates. The ego has not only to adjust the individual to the reality of life but also to protect him from all the unconscious demands and challenges of the superego and the id. The various mechanisms are called defences and usually function unconsciously. An analogy may be drawn with the means by which the body wards off infection, injury or foreign bodies. There is wide agreement among psychiatrists about these methods and they are worth mentioning.

Repression has been mentioned already and should be contrasted with suppression. Freud has been unjustly accused by those least acquainted with his work with the encouragement of a loose sexual code which makes no effort to curb either passion or desire. Whatever popular misrepresentation may have ensued, he himself was a man with high principles, devoted to his family and the last person to ignore the norms of conduct. His thesis was that there is a libidinal force in man which he needs to recognize and to come to terms with. When repressed, unneutralized, beyond the reach of consciousness, it behaves like an abscess which needs drainage. This is not applicable to suppression which is a conscious mechanism which we use to reject what may be immediately attractive and profitable but is against our welfare, spiritual, physical and mental. It is the commonest method with which the Christian will meet temptation, "put it out of his mind", at the same time seeking God's help to achieve this. Other mechanisms besides repression include denial, an unconscious disclaimer of a disagreeable situation; projection, attributing to others one's own obnoxious peculiarities; gossip about other people's alleged moral misdeeds and spiritual difficulties is a good example of this; identification, which is in some ways the opposite of projection for here we adopt qualities of others and accept them as the product of our own effort; substitution, as the name implies, allows us to canalize our inner anxieties and tensions in, for example, a physical symptom such as a headache, a pain or some form of disability, and psychosomatic disease is a branch of medicine which makes this province its own; reaction formations imply the development of a quality or trait opposing some strong unconscious desire, fear, or conflict, the extreme purist reacting against strong sexual urges, or the ultimate complication of adopting religion itself usually in its extreme form as a response to inner conflicts; rationalization: here real motives are concealed behind a fence of competently devised excuses, thus the dissatisfied husband works late because the work is excessive, the frigid wife refuses marital relations because of some bodily complaint and the alcoholic has business to conduct near the source of his liquor; finally, sublimation is the agency which allows the energy which flows from our unacceptable and forbidden instinctive life to be transformed along constructive channels to the higher realms of religion, art, literature and the wide range of socially and spiritually acceptable good works.

Freud, in brief, while not the originator of the concept of the unconscious, developed it to an unprecedented level. He was also able to establish the vital part of emotional experiences in subsequent human activity and its deterministic nature. That is to say, previous events in the life of a person could and did contribute to behaviour later on, which was meaningful when seen as a sequence of a life pattern of experiences including unconscious ones. These various contributions have been widely accepted in psychiatric practice. Later followers have criticized the strictly biological standpoint adopted by Freud and have modified some of his observations in the light of social and environmental factors. The Christian physician has also to modify them. Not only in the light of his own scientific training and experience and the belief, which he shares with others, that pleasure and gratification as an exclusive goal of human personality are untenable, but by re-echoing St Augustine: "Thou hast made us for thyself, O Lord and our heart shall not rest until it rests in thee." Furthermore, although he will allow, in special circumstances of marked abnormality, the diminution of free choice resulting from overwhelming emotions and, in some particular instances its total absence, these are instances of marked abnormality which do not violate the principle that for the majority of normal people the will is capable of making a free and deliberate choice according to the dictates of conscience, even if the optimal range may have been largely determined by the life pattern, conscious and unconscious, of the individual.

CARL GUSTAV JUNG (1875–1961)

From the very beginnings of psychoanalysis, disciples left Freud to pursue their own line of development. Jung, a Swiss psychiatrist, left the Freudians in 1913. He did not agree with the pan-sexual nature of libido. He retained the same word but extended it to represent all psychic energy. Besides this, there was also a clash of temperament and personality with Freud and in fact it was this which led Jung to a study of character types. The commonly accepted division of extroverts and introverts was the result of his work. The extrovert is the outgoing, sociable person finding his interests in people and things outside himself. The introvert, on the other hand, is shy and sensitive, unsure in company, diffident in interpersonal relationships, interested more in ideas than in people and things.

He also described four psychological functions: thinking, feeling, intuition and sensation. These may belong to an introvert or an extrovert personality which may use any or more than one of these functions as the dominant characteristic of communication with the world. The traditional absent-minded professor is the usual example given for the introverted thinker; artists may be either extrovert or introvert but lean heavily on their sensory experiences; the intuitive type will take a vast leap forward in the dark, disdainful of routine precautions and often against the dictates of discretion, achieving a triumph of imagination unattainable to the thinking plodder; while the feeling type is concerned primarily with human relations and values with a well-developed sense of their significance and need for fulfilment.

Jung subscribed equally with Freud to the presence of the unconscious but added that besides a personal unconscious unique to the person's experience there was also the collective unconscious, a deeper layer containing the experience of the race. This ability to experience current life by means of the past history of mankind Jung called archetypal and the postulated archetypes, although unconscious, are representative of the age-old experience of man. They reach consciousness in a variety of recurrent images. Fr White illustrates this and brings out with his example a fundamental difference in the approach between Jung and Freud.

Behind submerged "memories" of events in the individual's lifetime lies a racial heritage manifested in archetypal figures. Behind the particularized physical mother's womb lies the archetypal womb of the Great Mother of all living; behind the physical father the archetypal Father, behind the child the *puer aeternus*; behind the particular manifestation of the pro-creative sexual libido lies the Universal creative and recreative Spirit. The second of all these pairs appears now, not as a phantasy-substitute for the first; but rather does the first appear as a particular manifestation and symbol of the second. The way is now open to us, for instance, no longer to conceive of God as a substitute for the physical father, but rather the physical father as the infant's first substitute for God.[1]

Through the study of the collective unconscious, Jung reached the conclusion that besides sexuality and aggression there was in man a religious function of the utmost importance for the growth of the personality, which he neglected at his peril. In 1932 Jung wrote:

During the past thirty years, people from all the civilized countries of the earth have consulted me.... Among all my patients in the second half of life, that is to say over thirty-five, there has not been one whose problem in the last resort was not that of finding a religious outlook on life. It is safe

[1] Victor White, *God and the Unconscious*, Fontana Books, London (1960), p. 78.

to say that every one of them fell ill because he had lost that which the living religions of every age have given to their followers and none of them has been really healed who did not regain his religious outlook.[2]

For more detailed exposition of Jung, Christianity and psychotherapy the reader is referred to Fr Victor White's books, *God and the Unconscious* and *Soul and Psyche*.

ALFRED ADLER (1870–1937)

Another early pupil of Freud, Adler, dissented on the issue of sexuality as the all-pervading foundation for the development of personality. For him personality grew and was shaped by the individual's efforts to adapt to the needs of society to compensate for one or more inadequacies of his organism whatever form this took, physical, intellectual, emotional or social. To achieve this, the first line of approach was to make up the deficiency through work, a happy home and successful social relations, etc. If this failed, an exaggerated and neurotic effort may bring forth the assertive, bullying, petulant approach. An alternative opening is withdrawal to illness and self-pity, weapons with which the environment can be dominated. Adler postulated that the particular disease that emerged was not accidental but reflected a hereditary weakness of some organ which took on the brunt of the neurotic disturbance.

I. P. PAVLOV (1849–1936)

Pavlov was a contemporary of Freud working as a physiologist in Russia. All will be familiar with his famous experiments on dogs with which he was able to demonstrate that, for example, salivation as a natural response to food, which he called an unconditioned response, could be provoked after a time by any unrelated signal, such as a light or a noise, if the animal was trained sufficiently to associate the food or

[2] C. G. Jung, *Modern Man in Search of a Soul*, p. 264.

unconditioned stimulus with the conditioning stimulus whatever its character. A conditioned response was thus established
and the animal would salivate to the stimulus of a light, noise
or some other signal. His view of the development of personality was that this was simply an additive process with
the formation of suitable conditioned responses. The child's
character, entrusted to the hands of his parents and tutors,
grows by means of rewards and punishment which condition
his activities to meet the demands of his particular environment. Neurotic, pathological or immoral behaviour simply
result from maladaptive conditioning. Instincts and the unconscious, featuring so prominently in the dynamic schools
of personality, have no place here as causal agents in the
growth of personality. Although Pavlov and his followers
have been responsible for working out the details, the principles contained in their views have been the traditional basis
for the formation of good habits, development of character in
the layman's sense and society's hope of reclaiming the
criminal from time immemorial. There is little doubt they
contain much truth if incomplete as an exclusive explanation.

PSYCHOBIOLOGICAL CONTRIBUTIONS

Some workers, amongst whom Kretschmer[3] and Sheldon[4]
feature prominently, have insisted, with some success, that
there is a link between the personality and certain physical
characteristics. For example, Kretschmer has given the epithet
pyknic to the person who is of short stature, rotund figure,
with a broad face similar to the John Bull configuration. This
body build has been associated with an outgoing extrovert
personality, a tendency to changes of mood from depression
to elation and a close association with affective psychoses (see

[3] E. Kretschmer, *Physique and Character*, second edn revised, Miller,
London (1936).
[4] W. H. Sheldon and W. B. Tucker, *The Varieties of Human
Physique*, London and New York (1940); *The Varieties of Temperament*, London and New York (1942).

Chapter III). The leptosomic physique describes a tall thin person with a flat narrow chest. Introverts are predisposed to this type and there is some evidence to suggest that persons with this physical make-up are more often susceptible to psychiatric disorder including schizophrenia.

GENETIC FACTORS

While some schools will emphasize the genetic aspects more than others, all will agree that whatever the determining factors which may shape human personality subsequent to birth, each one of us arrives in this world endowed with a host of propensities, traits and characteristics which are genetically derived and represent the individual's inheritance from his parents and their respective lineal descent. The personality is then shaped in the battleground of nurture versus heredity. At the present moment there is much speculation but little definitive agreement regarding the respective contribution of each.

CHRISTIAN VIEWS

While it is imperative to incorporate all valid biological, and psychological contributions, for the Christian no theory of personality can be adequate or comprehensive which ignores the spiritual nature of man. His own distinctive contribution must be the impact of grace based on the primacy of love.

CHAPTER III

PSYCHOSES

PSYCHOSES

Psychiatric illness covers a wide range of disturbances. One group is characterized by gross abnormalities found in the brain and expressing themselves, for example, in mental defect, epilepsy and dementia. Another, the subject matter of this chapter, the psychoses, reveals no such gross features but nevertheless is accompanied by severe psychological derangement. The other major class is made up of the neuroses and personality disorders, which again reveal an absence of gross pathological features in the brain, but are nevertheless associated with a gradation of incapacity from the very severe to minor disturbances.

Psychotic illness expresses itself in a variety of symptoms in the realm of behaviour, thought, mood, emotion and in the capacity of evaluation and judgement. It can be easily appreciated that such defects are likely to be responsible for severe incapacity and, in practice, these are the conditions which, more than any others, express madness in the lay sense. The psychoses are subdivided into two main groups, schizophrenia and affective disorders.

SCHIZOPHRENIA

This condition, with an onset in the second, third and fourth decade, affecting the sexes equally, is characterized by disturbance of thinking, feelings, and behaviour and is usually accompanied by delusions and hallucinations. Its course is remittent but the progress of the disease for nearly seventy-five per cent[1] is towards deterioration and, since there is normally no shortening of the life expectation, schizophrenics tend to make up the single largest group in the chronic population of any mental hospital. Four types of schizophrenia are described, the simple, hebephrenic, paranoid and catatonic, exhibiting individually certain pronounced characteristics which help the differentiation, but generally following the same course.

In the simple type, there is an insidious deterioration of the behaviour. The person loses interest in his usual activities, withdraws from normal human relations even from his own relatives, showing an emotional blunting indicated by an indifference to events which appropriately would have evoked joy, mirth or sadness. He occupies himself with abstract subjects related to philosophy, religion or sociology, superficially appearing to be devoting his whole attention to these themes but in reality making little progress and gradually withdrawing further from any purposeful activity. There is a decline in study, work and the performance of religious duties with an attendant personal neglect in hygiene and health. The hebephrenic variety may depict some of these features but the principal disturbance here is disorder of thought. There is a looseness of associations in conversation, accompanied by vagueness, the introduction of new words and expressions, sudden thought blocking, together combining to render a piece of conversation fragmented and incomprehensible. The subject matter may have an extremely religious or sacred character and at times may give the appearance of a well-studied and deep sequence of thinking. To the thought disorder is usually added delusions, false beliefs not open to correction by reason or arguments, such as the staunch maintenance by the patient that he is Christ, God or some other important historical person, and hallucinations, sensory perceptions which have no basis and which are usually auditory.

[1] M. Bleuler, *Course of Illness, Personality and Family History in Schizophrenics*, Leipzig (1941).

For the sufferer these voices are real and he will vehemently defend them, sometimes declaring their origin to be of divine, angelic or a sacred nature, on other occasions imputing non-specific sources. The catatonic variety may have any of the above features but is usually characterized by stupor, a condition which has a generalized and marked reduction of activity, physical and psychological, as its main feature. Paranoid schizophrenia on an average has a later onset than the other three and the predominant feature is the presence of well-organized delusional systems in which the patient finds himself at the mercy of hostile and persecuting forces, sometimes known, often unknown to him, working for his ultimate damage, ill-health or utter destruction.

Despite much research, very little is known of the causes responsible for this disease. Genetic studies have clearly established that heredity plays an important part and this has been conclusively shown in studies of identical twins where, if the disease manifests itself in one of the pair of twins, then in nearly eighty per cent of cases the identical twin also succumbs sooner or later.[2] The previous personality may give a hint as it has been shown that nearly fifty per cent of these patients are solitary, shy, suspicious, unduly sensitive and in some way eccentric before the onset of the illness. Some physicians would stress that the ground is best fertilized for the seed of this disease in the early years of the infant child in disturbed and unsatisfactory interpersonal relations between the child and its parents. Whatever the ultimate explanation, and the likelihood of multiple factors is very high, at the present moment this disease is the commonest and effectively the most serious psychological illness.

The frequent close interest in religious, philosophical and mystical subjects and the presence of auditory hallucinations in this illness are issues of particular interest to the Christian community. Amongst candidates offering themselves for the

[2] F. J. Kallmann, *Heredity in Health and Mental Disorder*, New York (1953).

religious vocation, there is invariably a percentage who, in the course of time, will develop schizophrenia and will be unable to pursue their studies. It would certainly be advantageous to all concerned that no encouragement should be given to such a vocation which, with its attendant studies and enhanced personal obligations, may add a load sufficiently heavy to tip the balance adversely and precipitate the illness. Familiarity with the candidate's previous personal and family history may provide sufficient clues to put religious superiors on their guard and when in doubt to seek a competent psychiatric opinion.

Another, and at times even more challenging situation, is the claim of a person to have had a supernatural communication in the form of a vision or verbal message. Such claims are not infrequent and, in the careful assessment of cases, attention has always been paid, among other things, to the total functioning personality which in the case of schizophrenia will invariably offer some pathological evidence for the existence of an illness.

AFFECTIVE ILLNESSES

These form the other major group of psychiatric illness, characterized by a specific and marked change in the mood. Most people experience transient periods when their spirits are above or below par. When this state progresses to a prolonged and profound despondency or euphoria, depression and mania respectively set in.

Depression

This is by far the commoner of the two conditions affecting nearly one per cent of the population, women more than men, with a greater incidence in the upper strata of society and, unlike schizophrenia, appearing at a later age and reaching its peak in the sixth and seventh decades.

In a typical depressive illness, the main features are the marked changes in the mood, a quality of overwhelming misery replaces normal emotions, and is coupled with physical malaise. Patients feel that there is no further reason for living, hence the frequent suicide attempts. They are quite certain they have been abandoned by their relations, friends, the Church and Almighty God and this belief is justified by ubiquitous self-accusations of unworthiness, imperfections and past sins, real or imaginary. Neither encouragement nor reasoned explanation is of any help in the face of such self-destructive notions which are clear delusions. Unable to pursue their ordinary work, they sit or lie lamenting their state and remain preoccupied with their fate to the utter exclusion of ordinary interests and pursuits. Religious duties suffer with equal severity, the illness depriving the patient of his normal interest and ability to concentrate and execute the simplest of devotions. In addition to these severe mental manifestations, there are equivalent physical accompaniments with frequent episodes of weeping, loss of appetite and weight, inability to sleep and an overwhelming sense of fatigue. In this severe form, depressive illnesses constitute one of the most pathetic and sympathy-invoking sights in medicine. Before the introduction of electro-convulsive therapy, the duration of such an illness could extend over a period of six to nine months, but now it can be curtailed to a few weeks.

As with schizophrenia, despite extensive research, no satisfactory etiological factors can be incriminated so far, although heredity undoubtedly plays an important part, the incidence of this disorder being distinctly higher in the parents, siblings and children of those affected.[3]

The description given above indicates the condition in its most severe form, but not infrequently this severity is not attained and the suffering is not so disabling. Milder forms are related to a personal failure, family bereavement or disturbance, or social reverse, which has evoked more than the expected response of grief or disappointment but does not

[3] A. Stenstedt, "A Study in manic-depressive psychoses", Clinical, Social and Genetic Investigations, *Acta psychiat.* (Kbh), suppl. 79 (1952).

reach the extensive proportions of the malignant form. Sometimes, however, no such environmental factors are to be found and it is these situations that may lead to much misunderstanding and misery. The breadwinner, who is not obviously ill but nevertheless pursues his work reluctantly and less successfully, the housewife who finds her work endless, completes it partially and in a slovenly manner, may prove to be such examples. Both may find their religious zest shallower, prayer and religious duties a veritable cross, grudgingly performed, avoided or ignored. Their state, already virtually incomprehensible to their family, may be worsened by recriminations from the spouse or the well-meaning reproach of their pastor. Faced with the clear need to overcome their lassitude in their religious life, but quite incapable of making the effort, they may feel they are losing their faith. Their inaptitude may be interpreted as stubbornness, hardness of heart or indifference. It cannot be emphasized too much, both with regard to this condition and psychiatric illness in general, that wherever the behaviour of a person undergoes persistent changes inconsistent with previous behaviour or personality, which is inexplicable by changes in the circumstances of life, it is unwise to impute social or moral debasement in the absence of a clean bill of health, physical and psychological. A partially expressed depression is a condition which can account for some of these unexplained changes and bearing this in mind opens the way for the constructive proposal of a visit to a physician in psychological medicine.

Mania

This is a rarer disease affecting both men and women, in which the mood is elevated for a long period to an unprecedented and clearly pathological level. The person is gradually or suddenly overcome with a feeling of exhilaration and unprecedented joy. The tempo of life quickens, thoughts cascade through the mind and the victim is precipitated into hurried and ill-considered decisions, which are nevertheless considered to be of overwhelming importance. There is a mounting irritation but no sustained ill-will with all those who are unable either to comprehend the plans or share the quickened pulse of all the patient's activities. Communications with God and the saints may be claimed and so may special visitation or illuminations. Sexual activity is enhanced and individuals, who hitherto have upheld the highest standards of morality, will initiate and succumb to temptations utterly repellent, distasteful and incomprehensible to their relatives. Here indeed is a vital indication for hospital care during the attack, for in the absence of such protection, women may become pregnant in these circumstances. In addition, the incessant activity coupled with poor sleep and diminished food intake leads to exhaustion. Mania may alternate with depression in the same individual, but single attacks do occur. The outlook for the single attack is usually good.

SUICIDE

The successful termination of life by one's own hand has important theological, legal and psychiatric implications. The ancient world of the Greeks and Romans had mixed views on the subject but Plato, Aristotle, Virgil, Caesar, Ovid, Cicero, all condemned the practice in general although allowing specific instances. The Stoics appoved of it but this philosophical interpretation was not held widely. In the Christian era, St Augustine[4] clearly outlined the condemnation of suicide in the *City of God*. St Thomas[5] continues this tradition which has remained the teaching of the Church through the centuries to the present day. The grounds for this view are based on the commandment, "Thou shalt not kill", the concept that God is the author of life and man is the recipient of this gift, without any inherent rights of abrogation, which belong to God alone, the lack of any opportunity for repentance, and in its offence against the community which

[4] St Augustine, *City of God*, I, chapters xv–xxvi.
[5] St Thomas Aquinas, *Summa Theologica*, IIa–IIae, qu. 64 art. 5.

is thus deprived unjustly of one of its members. Suicide is thus a grave offence and when committed *deliberato consilio*, in the absence of insanity, ecclesiastical burial is denied (Canon 1240). The Anglican Communion denies full burial rites in similar circumstances. 1195329

The English law, taking its cue from these directives, ranks suicide as a felony and attempted suicide until very recently as a misdemeanour. Since August, 1961, attempted suicide is no longer an offence. This was the result of persistent criticism by medical and public opinion which saw no relationship between what is clearly, in the majority of these cases, an expression of illness and legal sanctions including the possibility of imprisonment.

The traditional sanctions on suicide have always been held subject to the exemption of those carrying out the act under the influence of mental illness. The two main groups of such disorders are schizophrenia and affective illnesses, especially depression. Depression is the single most important cause of suicide. There are on the average 5000 suicides in England and Wales and 17,000 in the United States a year, and between four to eight times this number of attempted suicides.

The last sixty years have seen extensive studies on this very important psychiatric subject. Research has come from two sources, the sociologists led by Durkheim,[6] who sought the cause in environmental social factors, and the psychiatrists, primarily interested in the psychological reasons. Durkheim's conclusions, since repeatedly verified, were that suicide was intimately associated with conditions where the links between the individual and a well-established cohesive community were loosened. He writes of "egoistic" suicide where this disintegration in family, political or social pattern leads to excessive isolation and individualism. Similarly, when the individual ceases to be subject to the laws and regulations of traditionally established customs, he refers to "anomic" suicide. These views were amply demonstrated in a study of

[6] E. Durkheim, *Suicide* (Eng. translation), London (1952).

suicides in London.[7] The medical author of this work found a close connection between suicide and social isolation, living alone or in a boarding house, social mobility, areas where the turnover of population was heavy, with high divorce and illegitimacy rates, and unemployment which was higher than in the average population. There was no significant relation to poverty *per se* or to overcrowding. Some of the features have been shown to apply in Eastern races. A study of suicide in Singapore[8] confirmed the relationship in the Chinese between suicide rates and size and stability of tribes, small and insecure tribes having a higher rate than the larger and more securely established. This work also revealed the impressively low rate amongst the Malayans who are Muslims, a feature shown by other Muslim communities.

Psychiatrists have concentrated on other important features. Thus all studies incriminate depressive illnesses, show a greater rate for men than women, and a rising rate with advancing age. This latter finding is tied up not only with the loneliness and dejection of old age but probably with physical ailments which in turn lead to mental illness. The exact incidence of mental disorder in suicide has been variously calculated between sixty to eighty per cent of all cases. Some psychiatrists hold the view that in all suicides the mind is disturbed, but this is not widely accepted. Apart from the sadness and misery of the affective illnesses, psychoanalytical theory sees in suicide an excess of aggression turned inwards in self-destruction.[9] Other features which have consistently emerged from various studies are the low rate of suicide in Catholic countries compared with Protestant ones, in rural districts compared with urban ones and in the married compared with the single.[10]

[7] P. Sainsbury, *Suicide in London*, Maudsley Monograph 1, London (1955).

[8] H. B. Murphy, "The Mental Health of Singapore, 1: Suicide", *Medical Journal*, Malaya (1954), ix, 1.

[9] Karl Menniger, *Man against Himself*, London (1938).

[10] W. Mayer-Gross, E. Slater and M. Roth, *Clinical Psychiatry*. London (1960), p. 227.

Recently attention has been given to the psychological factors operating in those who attempt suicide but are not successful. This group, numerically in excess of those who succeed, has a different composition being younger in age and with a predominance of women rather than men. One extensive study[11] sees all these acts as calls for help to the family at hand or to society as a whole. People, finding themselves at the end of their resources, exhausted of ideas or possibilities of securing help for their psychological, social or spiritual needs, resort to this last desperate means of securing attention. They do not desire death and this is shown by the manner of their suicidal attempt, the precautions taken to be near help and the ineptitude of the method used.

Analysing all these various characteristics, it is possible to reach certain conclusions. Suicide is a striking example to illustrate the beneficial impact of traditional Judaeo-Christian views on the importance of stable family and community life. Psychiatric and sociological work has revealed a host of new factors operating prior to the act of suicide. These have to be incorporated into Christian thinking as pointers for urgent consideration of how the would-be vicitim can be helped in modern society and also in the assessment of responsibility. A small proportion of suicides are the product of a calculated and clear act to avoid some social disgrace or personal tragedy and these would come under the objective censure of the Church. A large number would be adjudged clearly insane and exempted from any culpable responsibility. There is a minority where these neat divisions do not apply. The young sane woman, having no intention whatsoever of dying, who seeks help through an attempted suicide but miscalculates in her methods, resulting in death, is clearly not morally responsible for she neither anticipates nor intends death. If moral responsibility is to be judged solely on the criterion of insanity, a grave misjudgement can result.

[11] E. Stengel and N. G. Cook, *et al.*, *Attempted Suicide*, Maudsley Monograph 4, London (1958).

Again, in the absence of clearly defined insanity, a reassessment in terms of responsibility has to be made of the various social factors which, alone or in combination, may reduce sufficiently the freedom and judgement of an individual to the point of contemplating suicide, attempting it half-heartedly or successfully.

PUERPERAL MENTAL ILLNESS

The period immediately after childbirth is particularly susceptible for the appearance of psychological disorder. Before the modern era of antibiotics, infection was an important agent in causation. Nowadays this is no longer a problem and the incidence of these puerperal psychoses has diminished. There remains a risk, which is calculated as varying from one breakdown in 400 to 1200 pregnancies. The type consists mainly of either depression or a schizophrenic illness. These are both grave conditions, the first associated with an increased risk of suicide, and the second with the continuation of the condition needing hospital care. For both these reasons, various medical authorities have expressed the opinion that the previous history of such an illness is an indication for the termination of the next pregnancy. Some studies have come to gloomy conclusions about the prospects for recovery in these illnesses. Accurate information on this rare but important problem is not easy to come by as no adequate conclusions can be reached without a careful and sufficiently long period of follow-up to find out exactly the future outcome. One such study,[12] recently reported, has produced the most optimistic results to date. Seventy-five cases were studied with an average follow-up of four years involving 195 subsequent pregnancies. All the patients made a sufficiently good initial recovery to return home. Subsequently one in five had a recurrence with the next pregnancy. The study also

[12] M. E. Martin, "Puerperal Mental Illness, a follow up study of seventy-five cases", *British Medical Journal* (September 27th, 1958), pp. 773. (References to *British Medical Journal* hereafter *B.M.J.*)

showed that the predisposition to these illnesses on the basis
of inheritance was higher than in the population at large.

Although the result of this study has lifted some of the
apprehension surrounding these illnesses, it would not be
accurate to conclude that medical opinion has reached uniform agreement against terminating subsequent pregnancies.
Until more evidence is forthcoming, the Christian psychiatrist,
whose moral principles do not allow the termination of
pregnancy, is faced with a dilemma. With all patients, independent of their religious adherence, who express a wish
to continue with the pregnancy, his duty is to take adequate
safeguards to see they are not exposed to the serious risk
of suicide and to use the present adequate means of terminating a depressive illness. If asked, as he is likely to be,
about the prospects of a recurrence, he should be frank and
inform the patient on the basis of the available information.
If the background of a particular patient is unfavourable,
either in terms of heredity or the occurrence of repeated
illnesses, this would be a clear indication against further
childbearing, if this was the wish of the husband and wife
and, for Catholics, the justification for the permanent use
of the safe period. If more children were wanted, the same
safeguards would be taken at each pregnancy. There remains
the duty of the Christian psychiatrist whose patient does not
share his moral convictions. Under these circumstances he
must be scrupulously honest, state clearly his position and,
at the request of either spouse, be prepared to hand over the
management of the patient to a colleague.

CHAPTER IV

NEUROTIC AND PERSONALITY DISORDERS

In everyday language, the word neurotic is often used as a term of disparagement. A neurotic person is one who does not come up to the expectation or adequately meet the requirements of those with whom he has to relate and function. Depending on the relationship, proximity, ties of affection or hostility that hold him to others, he may be treated with sympathetic understanding, but inwardly labelled as inferior or second best, or become the recipient of cruel, derisive, rejecting and almost uniformly uncharitable comments and deeds. Contemporary society will accept the psychotic and mental defective with a mixture of fear and compassion, will recognize his illness but finds it difficult, with few exceptions, to accord a similar status to neurotic illness. There is an affinity to normality making it difficult or impossible to recognize symptoms as more than a refusal on the part of the person to "pull himself together". But this is precisely what, with a few exceptions, these sufferers cannot do. Nonetheless, these people are of average and very often above average intelligence, with ethical values in no way different from the rest of the community and not uncommonly providing a substantial core of highly artistic and gifted individuals.

The essence of a neurotic illness, for it is no less a pathological entity than other well-recognized categories, is the inability to meet and satisfactorily adjust to the demands of the environment either external or internal. Unlike psychotic illness, neurotics do not lose contact with the environment and the realities of life, they suffer none of the gross pathological features such as delusions and hallucinations and usually maintain a partial insight into their predicament. The cause of these disorders, like so much in psychiatry, is a matter of dispute with various schools making strong claims for their views. The Freudians see all neuroses stemming from inadequately resolved libidinal conflicts, which give rise to anxiety, which in turn is allayed by the various neurotic symptoms described below. Adler sees them as the product of the effort of asserting oneself by various neurotic compensatory means. For Jung they represent both negative aspects and a positive purpose. The symptoms are a warning of the lack of integration of all the elements of the personality but "the symptoms of a neurosis are not simply the effects of long past causes, whether infantile sexuality or the infantile urge to power, they are also attempts at a new synthesis of life—unsuccessful attempts let it be added—yet attempts nevertheless, with a core of value and meaning."[1] An emphasis which is shared in common by all is the importance of the early experiences in infancy and the need for satisfactory emotional environment, in particular with regard to the parents. Exponents at the other end of the scale will see these traits as genetically determined qualities with a normal distribution in the population, and the behaviourists, following closely on Pavlovian criteria, will see them purely as a manifestation of a maladaptive set of conditioned reflexes. All would agree that women are afflicted more often than men, the condition is commoner in the first half of life and that, although the rule is not general, there is usually a precipitating stressful situation. This may be an important decision, worries at home or work, adversity due to bereave-

[1] C. G. Jung, "Two Essays on Analytical Psychology", *Collected Works,* VII, p. 45.

ment, financial loss or great disappointment, sexual problems or a frightening, challenging or unpleasant situation.

What follows is a brief description of the main neurotic disorders with a fuller presentation of the obsessive-compulsive type which has particular significance in the Christian community.

HYSTERIA

This condition was first described by Hippocrates who treated it as an exclusively feminine ailment brought about by an abnormal wandering of the uterus. It is the earliest neurosis studied by Freud and since then it has had a distinguished list of commentaries by eminent physicians. Presumably by virtue of its ubiquity the term has been appropriated to serve as the generic colloquial term for branding the neurotic with the social stigma discussed at the beginning of the chapter. This is not surprising for it is a condition with dramatic and arresting features.

Although it may affect a man, the victim is usually a woman in her second, third or fourth decade, whose personality usually displays one or more of these features. Intelligence may be high or low, usually the former, behaviour tends to be childish, unstable, self-centred, unduly sensitive, capricious, irritable, with a well developed sense of dramatization and exaggeration. In the presence of an insoluble stressful situation, psychological forces come into operation bringing about a state of dissociation with an array of symptoms. Limbs may become paralyzed, the voice or vision lost, pain experienced or sensation lost and mental phenomena such as loss of identity or memory, inability to recognize relatives or familiar places, undue excitement or stupor may occur. To all this the patient may show appropriate concern but usually betrays an abnormal indifference and unconcern. This represents one frequent feature in hysteria, that of dissociation or the ability of the patient to function apparently adequately, with the exception of the pathological features which are separated and unintegrated. The operation of unconscious forces is held responsible for these disabilities. They prevent the patient from having to face the disagreeable situation, which he is avoiding, as well as offering usually some secondary gain such as attention and sympathy.

A point of some importance is the distinction between hysteria and malingering. In the latter case, a picture similar to hysteria may emerge under identical stressful situations but with the important difference that the person is consciously and deliberately imitating his symptoms to avoid the consequences of his actions. It is obvious that moral responsibility in these two instances will be entirely different. A note of warning should be added, however, that in practice there is an admixture of conditions and it may be extremely difficult to distinguish between the two. Successful treatment of a hysterical neurosis depends on the resolution of the underlying difficulties. It will easily be seen that this classical disease bears little resemblance to the popular concept and use of the word. Much nearer to that picture lies the histrionic personality which is a variant within the whole range of personalities and presents one or more of the features outlined. It is undoubtedly a source of much irritation to other people but clearly it is not a disease entity in the routine psychiatric sense although such people are a severe strain on their families, colleagues, doctors and pastors. In their spiritual life they tend to emphasize the dramatic and spectacular and unessential details on the fringe of their faith. They will choose and reject their confessors and spiritual directors on whimsical pretensions, lavish admiration on them and in no time renounce them with a host of unwarranted accusations. Not infrequently it is this personality which, hankering after the unusual, will see, discover and claim supernatural and miraculous intervention in the most unlikely circumstances. This is not to say that sanctity is not open to the histrionic person. God calls his heroic servants irrespective of their make-up. Discretion and careful assessment of each case are the invaluable safeguards against invalid claims and are particularly apt in these circumstances.

ANXIETY STATES

To be anxious is a state with which most people are familiar and which they have experienced at some time. It is an inner feeling of unpleasantness or uneasiness, accompanied frequently, but not invariably, by the physical symptoms of tightness in the pit of the stomach or in the head, with rapid and loud action of the heart, a dry mouth and sweating palms, spreading to intense agitation, acute fear and finally panic or flight. These are recognizable milestones of progressive responses in the face of threat or danger. The student before an examination, the candidate prior to his interview, the bride before her ceremony, the motorist who has just avoided a collision, the soldier in battle, the explorer unexpectedly encountering a wild animal, all these and a myriad of other circumstances will evoke anxiety, which, as can easily be seen in these predicaments, operates as a preparatory and protective device. It is when these feelings persist in situations in which no such response is called for, or an exaggerated one is evoked from a trivial triggering source, that we refer to abnormal anxiety states. These unhappy subjects live their lives in an aura of fear, feeling their work is not good enough although usually they are excellent employees, something of an unpleasant nature is expected to overtake their family at any time, their children's scholastic progress is a perpetual source of worry and sleepless nights are spent worrying over trifles of everyday life. While they do not seek deliberate attention, they need constant reassurance from any available source and this includes much encouragement in their spiritual life. When they have to face genuine crises, the pitch of anxiety may reach uncontrollable proportions and a pathetic figure pacing up and down, unable to eat or sleep, unamenable to any source of comfort, demands medical intervention and not infrequently hospitalization.

The prospects for complete cures are not high but much alleviation can be offered with a return to home and ordinary work.

PHOBIC STATES

This is a condition which, according to analytical interpretation, displaces latent anxiety not in the manner described above but to some object, person or idea which then becomes a target of morbid or irrational fear or apprehension. There are innumerable situations and objects which prudence and commonsense dictate should be avoided. Fears such as those of heights, darkness, thunderstorms, and crawling animals, to give only a few examples, are common enough not to attract undue attention. Some rare and unusual phobias can be traced back to a particular frightening experience in childhood, others perpetuate features present in either parent. When allowance has been made for these various possibilities, we are left with a residue which is, in the ordinary course of events, unexplainable. These are anxiety-provoking fears and include the inability to be left by oneself, to travel in buses or trains, to remain in an enclosed space (claustrophobia), to meet people, in the sexual sphere to meet members of the opposite sex, or after marriage to consummate it or to allow sexual relations. Much mental suffering accompanies the fear of contamination. Food, objects and people are suspected of being contaminated with bacteria and similar agents and a high level of hygiene is maintained for protection against these threats. Despite these precautions, there is a continuous painful anticipation, expecting to be struck by malevolent agents from any and all such sources. Reassurance and commonsense protestation are ineffective. If ordinary activities are curtailed to a standstill, hospital treatment may be required. It is the incomprehensible and markedly irrational nature of these fears that suggests unconscious motivation which in practice is found in a proportion of cases. When this is absent, strong hereditary traits predisposing the patient to these fears are postulated. But these explanations are not mutually exclusive.

OBSESSIVE-COMPULSIVE NEUROSES

This is one of the severest and most incapacitating neurotic illnesses. It usually starts between the age of fifteen to thirty and its chief characteristic is the patient's compulsive need to perform, think or imagine actions and ideas which he is actively resisting inwardly but cannot overcome. Children show slightly similar features in their games such as touching every alternate tree in the street, or hopping on alternate stones on the pavement. These habits are usually benign and do not preamble the adult illness. Symptoms in the adult may occur rapidly but usually it is a slow affair. Thus one patient, a commercial traveller, came too near a cyclist one day in his car and turned his head as he was passing by to check the safety of the cyclist. Seeing no mishap, he drove on. From that day onwards, the sight of any cyclist produced anxiety followed by the compulsive need to look back, irrespective of the existing traffic conditions. Soon he had actually to stop the car, get out and wait until the cyclist passed by. Not long after this, stopping once was not sufficient. Every time he overtook the same cyclist, the same proceedure had to be re-enacted. Within a year his job began to suffer since a journey which might normally take him twenty minutes was now stretched to one-and-a-half hours. Other common examples are rituals involving washing and dressing. Hands are washed not once but a dozen times or more and the morning toilet may take two or three hours to complete. Everything in the room from the clothes downwards must be handled in a particular manner and the slightest infringement of the sequence necessitates complete repetition. There are fears of dirt, which necessitate incessant washings, such as the handling of a door knob or a towel in a public institution, or of possible contamination from food items which are boiled over and over again to eliminate the threatening agent. Time taken to perform these activities makes heavy inroads into normal routine. The housewife finds little time for her ordinary duties, the business man is unable to complete his schedule, the clerk checks and rechecks *ad nauseam*, the student abandons his studies. In the mental sphere, the affliction is no less evident. There are obsessional ruminations with an image or sequence of ideas which keep on recurring to the exclusion of normal thoughts. This is an occurrence which may afflict anyone, when an idea, piece of music, or pictorial scene takes over for a time. When there is no relief at all, this becomes an obsessional rumination. The content of these may be complex or simple but they may be highly significant and painful such as the notion that a knife should be used to kill one's child or the certainty that somebody in the street will commit an obscene action. Indeed at times the sexual character may pervade right through and become unbearable. Obsessional sufferers are usually conscientious, precise people with high standards but usually rigid and inflexible with little capacity to adjust or alter.

The intimate link between this neurosis and scrupulosity is of great interest. If allowances are made for those with sensitive consciences or those with some particular spiritual difficulty on which they concentrate unduly but in accordance with reasonable dictates of their case, we are left with the scrupulous conscience. This is the Christian who, despite assurances, contrite confessions and impressive atonement, cannot find peace or lose the certainty that he has committed grave offences which have not been pardoned. He lives under the shadow of God's ire and contempt and the certainty of spiritual privation in this world and eternal damnation in the next. His prayers are long and arduous, the routine complicated and rarely does he come to a satisfactory conclusion of any section. He cannot attend Mass because of the certainty of divine wrath and cannot receive Holy Communion because of his unceasing doubts about his state of grace. He sees sin in all his activities. The most becoming of dresses becomes a source of worry because of the possibility of scandal and the most ordinary remarks are sources of persistent fears of misinterpretation. Confessors are changed after short periods of comfort and the vicious circle of uncertainty and doubts enlarges progressively, rendering spiritual peace impossible.

There is little doubt that some of these penitents are clear-cut cases of obsessional neurosis and should be advised to seek medical help with the pastor cooperating in the manner to be suggested in Chapter X. With cases that do not warrant such intervention the spiritual adviser should be aware that he is dealing with more than a theological problem. Thus the advice of putting the penitent under obedience may succeed but should not surprise either party if it does not. As with all neuroses, emotional factors are undoubtedly operating to a greater or lesser extent and these have to be appreciated before a comprehensive approach can be put into operation. It is possible that in some cases unconscious forces are present which demand this response as the only adaptive means of keeping a disintegrating personality intact. To abandon it might produce unbearable anxiety or even a complete breakdown. The exaggerated compulsive feeling of guilt is a pathological entity needing exploration along psychological lines and the confessional is certainly not the place to achieve this. Cooperation between doctor and priest in these instances offers a much greater hope for the management of these undoubtedly extremely difficult spiritual problems. Treatment is difficult and success by no means certain but recent studies[2] have indicated that the ultimate prognosis is not too gloomy with seventy per cent of patients able to lead a circumscribed but normal life.

Another issue in this disease is the matter of responsibility. In no other neurosis is the rational part of man and his

[2] J. Pollitt, "Natural History of Obsessional States", *B.M.J.* (1955), I, p. 194.

will subjected to such destructive forces and it is quite clear that in some cases, in the presence of unequivocal material infringement of the law, there is no formal imputability. This subject will be dealt with more fully in the chapter on responsibility.

PERSONALITY DISORDERS

So far in this chapter various neurotic illnesses have been outlined with delineated symptomatology, characteristics and courses. Attention has been drawn to the type of personalities which are vulnerable to the various diseases and by implication a difference has been drawn between the disease itself and the pre-existing personality. The predisposed personality may be present without the manifestation of the disease process and, after the active phase of the condition has cleared up, the person is still left with the same features and the same vulnerable propensities. The obsessional, anxious and histrionic personalities have been discussed. Three more deserve further consideration, namely the paranoid, immature or inadequate and the psychopathic personality.

Paranoid Personality

In the last chapter a short description of paranoid schizophrenia was given. Some of the features to be described presently would also be found in schizophrenia, with the difference that in this condition the person is in the grip of a severe destructive process, whereas the paranoid personality, despite many disadvantages, usually succeeds in remaining intact with regard to his home, social and spiritual life. The main features of this personality are undue self-centredness, sensitivity, egoism and mistrust of others. The paranoid person is continuously on the lookout for overt or covert slights aimed at him. Nearly everyone misunderstands him and he becomes a prey to a host of imaginary accusations which soon enough provoke real angry retorts from others. These only go to confirm the world of suspicion he has built round himself. Almost always isolated, he develops a stubborn response, entrenched in the alleged rights for which he is prepared to fight or to go to law. Cases of persistent litigation after all reasonable expectation has been exhausted represent well this type of disorder. Another feature is the occasional strong conviction that the person is the proud possessor of exclusive and all-important knowledge or belief. Founders of new religious sects and bizarre groups often attract similarly shy, lonely and vulnerable people, giving rise to strange associations sometimes ending in the further loosening of contact with reality and leading to psychotic breakdown. Religion is not infrequently the material with which paranoid people work. Their zeal, fanaticism and intolerance make them fitting subjects to outbid the living authority of the Church in condemnations and exaggerations of any tenet of the law to which they have particularly attached their interest. Thus strictures will follow behaviour which only by stretching the imagination could be considered improper and the theologian will condemn to eternal damnation those who infringe his criteria for salvation. Needless to say, logical explanations and arguments do no more than reinforce the convictions, adding the extra satisfaction of undertaking a fight for a lost cause. While contact in the business or social milieu provides an exacting experience for friends and associates, at least they can escape after a time. The family of such persons have no similar outlet and either suffer quietly or the marriage breaks up. When divorce is a permissible conclusion, not infrequently the first marriage is a prelude to a series as the same incompatibility re-emerges with the next spouse.

The uncertainty and insecurity of youth and old age are suitable breeding grounds for the emergence of such an outlook. Faulty vision or hearing in old age, the introspection of adolescence earlier on, or a handicap which draws attention to oneself may contribute at any period. Homosexuality has been instanced as a special abnormality associated with this condition and complex analytical explanations have been offered for this. It may be that homosexuality, with its legal and social sanctions, provides an ideal breeding ground for the development of this disorder. It is easily appreciated that the relatives and victims of paranoids will turn to the psychiatrist for help; typically, the sufferer himself rarely does. Unfortunately such entrenched characteristics are difficult to modify and success is not the rule, for the patient rarely sees the need either for treatment or for altering behaviour which for him is near enough perfect.

Immature and Inadequate Personalities

These entities are not so clearly delineated and often are labelled thus by a process of elimination. They do show however some features which are consistently present in a variable amount. In this particular context, the word mature is used with reference to emotional maturity. Thus an emotionally mature person is one whose needs have outgrown the childhood dependence on parents and figures of authority, who is able to exchange love and security on equal terms with others, who can form stable and lasting relationships, can experience suffering without succumbing, feel anger and hatred with reasonable control over both. While it is clear that such a balanced blend is an ideal rarely accomplished, most people manage to achieve a fair success even if they have their own particular Achilles' heel to guard against. The immature personality shows weakness and limitation on a broad front. Unable to meet the demands of conjugal exchange, he may remain under the umbrella of parental protection, or may seek a spouse who will fulfil the needs of the inadequacy, taking most decisions and virtually continuing the parental rôle. One meets not infrequently the dominant partner of such an emotionally barren match, weary and exhausted in the rôle of support, sexually dissatisfied, translating the frustrations into a host of physical complaints. Although passive dependence may go some way to meet the needs of the emotionally immature, there is often an undercurrent of dissatisfaction with their own lives. Fearful of their own anger and the rejection of those on whom they depend, their irritation is communicated in an unceasing warfare of veiled hostility. Petulant, contentious, difficult to please, they meander through life unable to fulfil or be fulfilled. Their work shows the same instability, and fear of responsibility. Irked by authority, incapable of perseverance, they may find a niche with a sympathetic employer or may drift from job to job, sinking in the social strata to petty crime and prostitution. With their peculiar emotional limitation, these personalities are particularly prone to the tempting if temporary reassurances of drink and drugs.

While in some cases successful rehabilitation is achieved by examining the psychological causes, both conscious and unconscious, which have contributed to what amounts to psychic infantilism, very often the best that can be achieved is long term support for the patient and his relatives, especially at times of crises. Often the patient's childhood will reveal the absence of a stable, loving background, a combination of a strict and rigid father with an indulgent but ineffective mother or a cold, rejecting mother with an ineffectual father. Sometimes parents may protract the dependence of their children on them to serve their own unconscious needs. Other etiological factors include the individual's ontological adverse experiences such as painful or protracted illnesses, educational backwardness, or competition with siblings endowed with greater gifts.

Psychopathic Personality

In 1835 an English physician named Prichard coined the term "moral insanity".[3] He was the first physician to describe this type of personality characterized by intellectual faculties

[3] J. C. Prichard, *Treatise on Insanity*, London (1835).

which are preserved unaltered but accompanied by marked derangement of feelings, temper or habits. As moral insanity implies, the defect is one of personal conduct which has a marked antisocial element. All the ordinary rules of conduct are flouted and such persons give vent to tempers, dishonesty and violent acts without the slightest sense of committing wrong, the need for reparation or the intention to amend.

From early childhood and in a home which has consistently been shown to have well above the average proportion of parental separation, discord, alcoholism or in some way incapable and rejecting parents, there is evidence of psychopathy. Lying, disobedience, truancy, petty thieving all gradually develop. With adolescence, the remnants of any form of submission to authority are rejected and this trend accentuated. Behaviour becomes impulsive, frustration of any sort is met with instantaneous, violent and often aggressive behaviour. Psychopaths are unable to settle to routine, change their jobs frequently and unreliability is a constant feature. Promises are made solemnly and broken immediately, good intentions are proclaimed and abandoned with every subsequent action. Anxiety as a self-controlling and inhibiting influence is rarely experienced. While aggression is frequent, it is not essential and the smooth and suave confidence trickster with his ability to spin plans full of wonders, fantasy and trickery belongs to this group. Endowed with average or above average intelligence and much superficial charm, they make rapid friendships which are shallow and often the graveyard of financial and matrimonial arrangements for those swept away by such promises. Not only are they incapable of giving anything but they can be cruel to the extreme and sexually intolerant of any prohibition. In short, conscience is a word that is foreign in its entirety as is the ability to learn from experience. Theories of possible causation abound but informative facts are few. One feature that is a relatively constant finding, other than the home conditions, is that the electrical recordings from the brains of such people show evidence of immaturity to a degree well above that expected in a population of similar age.[4]

As can be easily imagined, these personalities feature constantly in court,[5] in the psychiatric hospital and in the matrimonial courts, both civil and ecclesiastical. Until very recently the condition had no formal footing in the eyes of the law but the Mental Health Act of 1959 recognizes this type of psychopathy as a disease entity which may justify the detention of these individuals against their will to be treated in special units. Treatment to date is extremely disappointing and, apart from protecting the individual against falling a prey to drug addiction, alcoholism, organized crime and prostitution, there is little that can be achieved in radically modifying these traits. Time, however, seems to be a favourable agent and there is a tendency for a diminution of the excesses and the introduction of some stability with the second half of life. It is in connection with this type of patient and the variety who consistently transgresses the sexual *mores* that at least one country has introduced castration as a treatment. The moral implications of this step are discussed in the chapter on treatment.

The psychopath features frequently in courts, various studies finding an incidence of seven to twenty per cent[6,7] of convicted offenders. The complex issues offer a meeting ground for the psychiatrist, penologist and moral theologian. The physician, finding no symptomatology of psychiatric disorder, no delusions, hallucinations, illusions, neurotic manifestations, mental deficiency or brain damage, has long eschewed the task of adding this condition to psychiatric illness proper. Sociopathy yes, but psychopathy no, is still

[4] D. Hill and D. Watterson, *Journal of Neurological Psychiatry* (1942), v, p. 47.

[5] S. S. Glueck and E. T. Glueck, *500 Criminal Careers*, New York (1930).

[6] W. Bronberg and C. B. Thompson, *Journal of Criminal Law and Criminology* (1937), xxvii, p. 1.

[7] B. Glueck, *Mental Hygiene*, ii, p. 85, New York (1918).

the view of eminent commentators.[8] Punishment of any sort is singularly unreformative and the courts in despair turn to the psychiatrist for guidance. He in turn can only offer the least satisfactory alternative, detention for an indefinite period. And for the moral theologian the situation presents a quandary. In the presence of cognitive integrity and unimpaired reason, it is nevertheless clear that in a good few cases conscience, here defined as the antecedent ability to choose between right and wrong and the consequent capacity to appreciate the rightness or wrongness of an action, lacks proper if any formation. Responsibility is accordingly diminished and may vary from non-existence to substantial reduction depending on individual circumstances. Another feature is the disparity between the strength of the instincts and the constitutional weakness of the will power. This further diminishes responsibility for individual actions. These features have also been incorporated in criminal responsibility, for the concept of irresistible impulse as grounds for reducing responsibility has been accepted by English Law.

A slightly different but equally important issue is the psychopath's inability to evaluate the consequence of his actions. We have seen how the psychopath is not only unable to distinguish social and moral values but often proves unreliable in the content of his promises with his habitual indifference to repair, restitution or any solemn intent. Thus the freedom of action although apparently intact is gravely impaired. This is an issue which confronts ecclesiastical courts in matrimonial cases. Freedom in matrimonial cases refers to the absence of any coercion in the act of the will which wills to marry and to marry one certain person. Freedom, in the sense it is used here, is tied up with the ability of the person to implement the verbal expression, despite his appearance of normal rationality and full knowledge. In some cases, it can be shown from the evidence of previous

[8] A. Lewis, "Health as a Social Concept", *British Journal of Sociology* (1953), IV, p. 2.

conduct that this is so unlikely as to take it out of the range of reasonable expectation. While it is not invariably so and each case needs extremely careful assessment, the author is of the opinion that in some cases the psychopath's matrimonial vows are invalid and offer grounds for the nullity of marriage. Thus, if they promise to love and cherish their spouse until death and the same day or a few days later leave them for someone else, it is difficult to accept such promises at their face value. Equally, if a wealthy match is concluded and the same pattern is followed the moment the wealth is acquired, in a person with such a character it is equally certain that the promises are in fact rendered meaningless.

CHAPTER V

SEXUAL PROBLEMS

Of all the developments in modern psychiatric thought subsequent to Freud, the sexual theory easily heads the list in
provoking the greatest disapproval and mistrust. This is
not surprising, for even where it trespasses neither on dogma
nor traditional teaching, it impinges on a Christian area
of thought which has yet to resolve satisfactorily its own
innate conflicting forces. There are in Christian tradition two
commanding but independent views which have yet to be
reconciled. On the one hand, there is the line of thought
followed by, to quote only two eminent figures, St Gregory
of Nyssa and St Augustine. St Gregory, while recognizing
sexuality as an essential part of creation, maintains that this
is only so because God foresaw original sin and its consequence, death. If man had not fallen, there would have been
no death, nor any need for sexuality in its present form,
hence the intimate link between sin and sex. St Augustine,
pursuing a similar line, has left an indelible and rigorous
interpretation of sex in Christian life. Not wholly unconnected
with his own previous experiences and influenced by the
Manichean beliefs he once held, he concentrated on the view
that concupiscence or sexual appetite constituted an essential element of original sin and that it is transmitted in
generation which invariably needs concupiscence. St Augustine was thus inclined to the view that the sexual act in
marriage was always accompanied by evil except when

the act was specifically intended to procreate.[1] St Thomas, on the other hand, sees nothing essentially wrong either in sexual desire or relations which, even in the absence of original sin, would have still existed. Thus for him sexual generation was part of the original plan for man[2] but sin has placed this passion along with others beyond his smooth and perfect control. One can thus discern two broad configurations taking shape, one relatively optimistic, the other pessimistic, on the nature of human sexuality. On the whole, it has to be admitted that the latter approach has figured more prominently and the dilemma, by no means a simple one, awaits resolution and integration. In practice the path of personal continence, celibacy and virginity in the service of God has been accepted as the ideal, marriage as a sacramental state second in excellence. All concur that sexual aberrations are abhorrent deviations deserving the severest censures. Undoubtedly part of this approach has the imprint of an exaggeration which is emotionally and culturally determined and which does justice neither to the theological nor social implications of the individual circumstances. In this chapter we shall examine some such implications in the content of modern psychiatric developments.

HOMOSEXUALITY

By homosexuality we refer to the orientation of sexual desire towards persons of the same sex. This is a condition with a very long history. Jewish tradition condemned this practice, drawing this conclusion primarily from the account of Genesis 19. 4–8. Two angels visited Sodom and Lot invited them to his house.

> But before they went to bed, the men of the city beset the house, both young and old, all the people together. And

---

[1] *Conjugalis concubitus generandi gratia, non habet culpam; concupiscentiae vero satiandae, sed tamen cum conjugae, propter thori fidem, venialem habet culpam* (*De bono conjugali*, cap. VI).

[2] *Summa Theologica*, ıa, qu. 98 art. 2.

they called Lot and said to him, Where are the men that came into thee at night? Bring them hither that we may know them. Lot went out to them and shut the door after him and said: Do not do so, I beseech you, my brethren; do not commit this evil. I have two daughters who as yet have not known man: I will bring them out to you, and abuse them as it shall please you so that you do no evil to these men, because they are come under the shadow of my roof.

As a punishment for their evil intentions Sodom was destroyed. The Anglican theologian, Dr D. S. Bailey, has challenged the interpretation of this episode in his scholarly book *Homosexuality and the Christian Tradition*. Homosexual practices are further condemned in Leviticus 18. 22: "Thou shalt not lie with mankind as with womankind, because it is an abomination," and further on, Leviticus 20. 4: "If anyone lie with a man as with a woman, both have committed an abomination, let them be put to death. Their blood be upon them." Christianity, following in this tradition, also condemned such practices, beginning with St Paul's Epistle to the Romans (1. 26–7): "For this cause, God delivered them up to shameful affections. For their women have changed the natural use into that use which is against nature. And, in like manner, men also, leaving the natural use of the women, have burned in their lust one towards another, men with men, working that which is filthy and receiving in themselves the recompense which was due to their error." The Fathers were equally disapproving and the words of St Augustine set the tone of the reaction to such behaviour. In his *Confessions* he writes: "Even if all nations committed such sins, they should all alike be held guilty by God's law which did not make men so that they should abuse each other thus. The friendship which is between God and us is violated when nature, whose author he is, is polluted by so perverted a lust." St Thomas Aquinas also held that such actions were contrary to reason and contrary to the natural order of the sexual act which has procreation as its primary aim. In the context of these condemnations it was inevitable that homosexuality should be seen as a deliberate perversion, an obstinate rejection of normal sexual desire and conduct in favour of a particular detestable practice. By implication it is understood that this is a free choice which persists despite admonition and is an expression of an evil and vicious will deserving severe punishment which in former times amounted to death.

Some of the ferocity of the early edicts may be accounted for by the high incidence of homosexuality in the ancient Greek and Roman world. With their overvaluation of sport, the appreciation of a finely proportioned athletic body, the relative devaluation of women and the presence of male slaves, it is not difficult to see that for the Greeks the love of one man for another became the occasion of a noble experience, the source of poetic and manifold artistic expression. Such affection was profound, sincere and found its outlets much more often in tokens of friendship, in contrast with Roman practices which prized sensuality. Rapidly traversing the centuries to reach our own times, anthropologists have found it present in various primitive communities which have been studied. Some of these approve of it, others condemn it and some are indifferent. Our own attitude is anything but indifferent and it is true to say that, for Great Britain and the U.S.A., this deviation receives society's full measure of censure and opprobrium. Prostitution, crime and cruelty are all disapproved of but allowances are made, but in most eyes the sin of Sodom is the unforgivable one. All links with such a contamination amount nearly enough to social and moral leprosy.

What is the incidence of this condition? Before we search for the figures, it is essential to clarify that this is not an either/or condition. Fundamentally all of us are potentially capable of being homosexual, although some evidence suggests that some are more prone than others due to hereditary factors. To this we shall return when we discuss possible causes. Meanwhile we have to accept the overwhelming evidence that this is a state which has a variable hold. There are those exclusively heterosexual, with all trace of homosexuality extinct; those who are heterosexual in normal circumstances but who, under stress of war or isolation in prison or concentration camp, have homosexual adventures; the relatively few who are bisexual; and finally the exclusive inverts. It is the last category, the group who know no other sexual feeling or outlet and who are repulsed by normal attractions, that forms the centre of this immensely difficult problem. Various previous calculations have been superseded by the two Kinsey reports. These findings have been criticized, often savagely, by those who find the contents esthetically disagreeable and choose to ignore them when the figures do not suit their preconceived notions. The fact is that all medical studies can be criticized in some detail but provided that the basic work ignores no important scientific criteria, the results can be accepted with any necessary reservations. The Kinsey reports have been so acknowledged and, even if they carry some experimental error, none of the major conclusions has been validly disputed. Dr Kinsey confined himself to overt physical sexual contact, and the population is drawn entirely from the U.S.A. The figures for the confirmed invert shows an incidence of four per cent for the male and less for women.[3] Up to the age of forty-five at least thirty-seven per cent of men had had some homosexual contact although mostly a passing one, while for women this figure was only thirteen per cent. Lesbians tended to remain true to their companion, men tend to have numerous associations. Religion was a factor and devout adherents of Catholicism, Protestantism and Judaism showed a lower incidence.[4] These figures are certainly startling

[3] A. C. Kinsey, W. B. Pomeroy and C. E. Martin, *Sexual Behaviour in the Human Male*, London and Philadelphia (1948), p. 651.

[4] A. C. Kinsey, W. B. Pomeroy, C. E. Martin and P. H. Gebhard, *Sexual Behaviour in the Human Female*, London and Philadelphia (1953), p. 463. (The lower incidence applies to the findings for the male as well.)

and if the incidence in Great Britain is of the same order, and there is no evidence to suggest the contrary, then there are nearly one million inveterate male homosexuals in that country. The social, legal and religious implications assume dimensions which cannot be dismissed as the "wicked few".

If we move from numbers to causes, we shall find a plurality of explanations. Some adhere to the view that these traits are inborn, and inheritance with its specific predisposition is the operative cause. In its support this theory claims the results of one of the leading psychiatric geneticists, who investigated eighty-five sets of twins, forty identical and forty-five non-identical. Since both types of twins are subjected in a family to the same kind of environment, if it is found that the expression of a condition is greater in the identical variety who have inherited an exactly similar type of genetic make-up, then this is good evidence to suggest that inheritance and not upbringing plays the dominant rôle. Kallmann,[5] to whose study I refer, traced thirty-seven of the identical twin brothers all of whom were homosexual as compared with only three of the ordinary twins. This is a striking finding which, if confirmed in a differently selected group, would go a long way to tip the balance in favour of this view. Others, not unnaturally, have concentrated on the hormonal make-up of these patients, for it is well known that hormones play a significant rôle in our sexual make-up. Both sexes have some of each other's hormones but oestrogens predominate in women and androgens in men. Some workers have claimed to have found an excessive amount of the former in these men and hold this finding responsible for the state. Apart from the fact that others have not confirmed their results, in practice female hormones have been used to treat certain ailments in men in quite heavy doses without

[5] F. J. Kallmann, "Comparative Twin Study of the Genetic Aspects of Male Homosexuality", *Journal of Nervous and Mental Disorders* (1952), cxv, p. 283; "Twin Sibships and the Study of Male Homosexuality", *American Journal of Human Genetics* (1952), iv, p. 136.

any material alteration in the sexual outlook of the patient. The general conclusion in this matter seems to be that, while appropriate hormones may be responsible for intensifying sexual desire, they play little part in the choice of the love object. Biological explanations, with the exception of the unconfirmed but important finding of Kallmann, are meagre up to the present. Turning to psychological ones, we start with the orthodox Freudian view. The oedipal complex is the kernel of the enigma. This is the stage when the child is attracted towards the parent of the opposite sex, the mother in the case of the boy. Such a sexual pull encounters considerable guilt and anxiety, unconsciously, but retains a coercive restraint in adult life, rendering an approach to women impossible. Alternatively, the pull towards the mother is so overwhelming that in the presence of a weak, callous or indifferent father, the boy identifies his sexual interest with the feminine passive rôle. Even if this analytical interpretation lacks conviction, the fact remains that an excessive attachment to the mother in the presence of an ineffective or hostile father is a very frequent finding, confirmed by workers adhering to no particular school of thought.[6] Other factors which might contribute are an upbringing in an entirely female atmosphere, rivalry with a sister who is getting favourable attention and with whom her brother can only compete by imitating her, and sometimes a dominant and clinging mother who is determined to keep her boy her own.

Many people are unduly worried about the risk of seduction as a means of contaminating the young. Despite insistent accounts by homosexuals that their life changed after such an incident, there is little evidence in favour of this. In one study[7] carried out on 100 Borstal boys between sixteen and twenty-one as many non-homosexuals had been so attacked

[6] D. J. West, "Parental Relationship in Male Homosexuality", *International Journal of Social Psychiatry* (1959), v, p. 85.

[7] T. C. N. Gibbens, "The Sexual Behaviour of Young Criminals", *Journal of Mental Science* (1957), CIII, p. 527.

as homosexuals. Much more important is the provision of heterosexual outlets where boys and girls may meet and develop a mutually healthy attraction and respect. The all-male atmosphere of boarding schools may enhance homo-erotic proclivities. In this connection it is well known that adolescents and young people with an excess of sexual energy do, in the process of discovering their own potentialities, indulge in such activities. The "crushes" on teachers and the leaders of the school are well known and in the majority of cases are only transitional phenomena. So are active sexual practices which at this stage present no more than another possible outlet to the rich range of awakening physical gratification. It is not customary to attach the homosexual label to people under twenty-five although in some cases it may be abundantly obvious that no change can be expected.

Shy, diffident people, already uncertain of themselves, may have an affair with the opposite sex which is unsuccessful and humiliating. If they are already under the umbrella of a mother, who is anxiously watching this first heterosexual exodus, her sympathy and over-protection may make it the last. Any atmosphere which treats sex severely, emphasizes its dangers and undervalues the fruits of heterosexual love may disincline such a person from further experimentation, slowly establishing the pattern of a passive homosexual rôle, relying on safety of the kind it knows and understands. In our present state of knowledge, psychological factors are considered paramount, stressing the vital rôle of the mother and the need to clear away as many obstacles as possible to heterosexual paths.

Treatment is often recommended by the courts, pastors or employers. It is sought less often by the invert himself, except to comply with and thus escape society's threats of punishment. Very often the homosexual, although desirous of a more tolerant attitude from those around him, is nonetheless content with his own inclinations and is not anxious to change them. Such cases, and they are the majority, seek no help and none is available. There are those who, because of social and moral pressures, feel they should make the effort but inwardly reject the attempt; once again treatment offers no reasonable hope of success. Even with the right intentions, it has to be admitted that the majority of exclusive homosexuals are unlikely to change their orientation towards heterosexual habits. Psychoanalysis claims such successes and undoubtedly achieves a number. These probably represent individuals with latent heterosexual feelings which are not beyond recall. This is a lengthy treatment and care must be taken to select suitable candidates. For the rest, and this really applies to the majority, psychiatry, while unable to alter the basic outlook, can help them to restore self-confidence, allay excessive guilt, which is often neurotic in character, assist them in accepting their state and utilizing their potential for a creative, useful life in accordance with their moral norms. The homosexual is the recipient of much antagonism, mistrust, prejudice, and often at the mercy of blackmail and calumny from a society which has an excess of ignorance and a minimum of charity. It is not surprising that such forces, which have combined to make these people outcasts, will produce disagreeable psychological effects and it is the psychiatrist's task to untwine the environmentally produced knots and free, as far as possible, the victim from neurotic conflict, whatever the source of its origin.

It may well be asked how can this be accomplished when the invert sins against his nature. I hope it has become abundantly clear that the state itself carries no stain of sin and offends neither God nor society. If this alone became clear in the minds of people, the homosexual's lot would ease immediately. If he can lift his head and present himself on equal terms with others, some of his problems would be resolved. Not all, because, if he practises the Christian faith, he is still expected to resist all physical sexual contacts. But he would be free to concentrate on this and strengthen his efforts, in no way dissimilar from all those whose passions are strong. Even then, the man will not have the natural outlet of marriage, the support and affection of his family. But the grace of God abandons no one. If he can feel secure in the love of God, the friendship of his pastor and society, he can concentrate on offering himself to his Creator and his services to the community. Since he possesses no innate evil, he deserves to be treated not as a perverted outcast but as a citizen no less worthy than others.

At present he risks constant humiliation, loss of employment, blackmail and imprisonment. Homosexual practices between adults, even privately, incur the risk of prosecution and, to show that this is no empty threat, the Wolfenden Report[8] disclosed that for the three years ending March 1956, 300 adult offenders were convicted solely for offences committed in private with other consenting adults. Of these, 116 were sent to prison, sentences ranging from twelve months to a maximum of five years. The Wolfenden Report recommended that homosexual acts between consenting adults over twenty-one (females are not prosecuted) should be made legal but this suggestion was rejected by Parliament. To send the homosexual to prison when society ignores adultery and fornication seems grossly unjust. The hope of any reform in the all-male atmosphere of prison, and in the presence of the hostility and justified resentment of the offender, has been compared with the chance of rehabilitating the alcoholic by giving him work in a brewery. The protection of the community is not at stake and in any case adequate safeguards can be taken against the distinct minority who seek to deprave the young. Both the Catholic Church and the Church of England were asked to give their views before the Wolfenden Committee. Their conclusions, reached independently, are virtually identical. The report of the Roman Catholic Advisory Committee on Prostitution and Homosexual Offences and the existing Law was published in the *Dublin Review* of Summer

[8] Wolfenden, "Report of the Committee on Homosexual Offences and Prostitution" (1958), H.M.S.O., Cmd. 247.

1956. It outlines the position of the Church, confirms the essential immorality of homosexual acts but, with regard to the law, goes on to say:

> The existing law does not effectively distinguish between sin, which is a matter of private morals, and crime, which is an offence against the State, having antisocial consequences. Under the existing law, criminal proceedings against adult male persons in respect of consenting homosexual acts in private (whether of the full offence of sodomy or of gross indecency) inevitably fall upon a small minority of offenders and often upon those least deserving punishment. It is accordingly recommended that the criminal law should be amended in order to restrict penal sanctions for homosexual offences as follows, namely, to prevent: (a) the corruption of youth, (b) offences against public decency, (c) the exploitation of vice for the purpose of gain. It should be clearly stated that penal sanctions are not justified for the purpose of attempting to restrain sins against sexual morality committed in private by responsible adults. They should be discontinued because (a) they are ineffectual, (b) they are inequitable in their incidence, (c) they involve severities disproportionate to the offence committed, (d) they undoubtedly give scope for blackmail and other forms of corruption.

MASTURBATION

Self-stimulation of the genitalia or adjacent area with the specific aim of obtaining venereal pleasure is a practice which Christianity in general condemns. Catholicism rates such deliberate acts as grave or mortal sins. Since they occur extremely frequently, they are a source of great anxiety to pastors, parents, the young people themselves but of relatively little significance to psychiatrists not directly involved with the moral issues. They see such behaviour as a biological phenomenon, a well-nigh universal accompaniment of adolescence for the man, with a relatively smaller incidence for the girl. It is one of the very few issues in which physicians find it very hard to share the anxieties exhibited by everyone else and accordingly a subject which is likely to get the least sympathy if a similar ethical outlook is not shared. The spiritual adviser, on the other hand, who views all such acts with the apprehension warranted by a grave offence, is anxious to do all he can to help his flock and is frequently facing an apparently impossible situation for, hard as he may try, for a time the habit appears entrenched and insurmountable. Once again we resort to Dr Kinsey for figures and he shows that by the age of twenty, ninety-two per cent of men and nearly forty per cent of women have masturbated. Any priest familiar with parish work and all psychiatrists would not be in the least surprised by these figures. The frequency abates with increasing age and in marriage it is understandably a rare occurrence. Adherents of faiths which condemn this practice show a lower incidence.

The young child of two to five, in the process of familiarizing himself with his body, will certainly carry out manœuvres which superficially appear to be masturbatory in character. The exact meaning of these occurrences to the child is not altogether clear although they appear pleasurable. Parents, haunted by the spectre of sex, will often mirror in their interpretation and reactions their own fears and anxieties. What is absolutely certain is that these activities are perfectly innocent, morally and physiologically, and that the ideal response for the parents is either to ignore them or, if this is not possible, to share in suitably explanatory terms the discovery of their child. It is never too early to build up and communicate by every possible means the notion that the body is good, holy and the temple of the Holy Spirit.

With the advent of puberty and adolescence, both sexes are seized, physically and psychologically, with the vibrations of sexuality. Life is visibly altered not only in the shape and function of the body, but in the relationship with parents, teachers and members of the opposite sex; established friendships are loosened and new ones established with intensities which betray the underlying uncertainty. Disequilibrium and insecurity prevail, coupled with strong biological urges. The young person is finding himself or herself in an entirely new rôle and part of the discovery is sexual pleasure. While this description applies to the majority, masturbation can be a symptom of a more sinister condition. Morbid deviations in personality, unsatisfactory environmental conditions at home, school or work, compulsive elements, psychotic illness, any one of these may aggravate this practice, but now we are dealing with a complex and abnormal situation which needs psychiatric help. For the average person, such intervention is totally unwarranted and psychiatrists unceasingly reiterate that no one has shown any deleterious effects from this practice. Conflict between the wish to observe the moral law and the need to satisfy these desires will vary according to upbringing and temperament. Such consequent guilt certainly does not warrant a medical visit and is the occasion, *par excellence*, when the spiritual adviser can and should be able to help. Persistent masturbation in adult life presents a different issue, for while it may be the sole outlet for the homosexual or the symptom of a compulsive neurosis, it often belongs to a constellation of neurotic maladjustment.

SADISM AND MASOCHISM

The term sadistic is used extensively and with a wide range of meanings but most, if not all, approach the essence of cruelty. In its strict psychiatric sense, it connotes the derivation of sexual pleasure from acts and thoughts which are aggressive and inflict suffering on others. This need not always be physical, very often it is mental in character. Sadism is much more commonly associated with male behaviour but it is known in women. Although extreme sadistic behaviour is rare, on a smaller scale it is more frequent than is commonly supposed. Psychoanalytic theory explains it by associating libidinal energy with the innate aggression postulated as present in all human beings. Whatever the explanation, it is an indisputable fact that sexual drives can be canalized along this route and it is a potentiality that cannot be dismissed or ignored by anyone, especially by those who have authority and charge over others. The literature is littered with descriptions of sexual arousal in childhood by the infliction of punishment by parents and tutors, especially on persons of the opposite sex. In schools, it is essential to guard against the exchange of discipline for an emotionally motivated dialogue between the inflicter and the victim. It is sufficient to keep in mind the possibilities to avoid excesses but, if unconscious incentives are dominating, it may be difficult to assess one's conduct with any useful insight. While the physical components of sadistic behaviour are necessarily confined to those situations where force is a weapon of human behaviour, these of their very nature are not widespread. Intellectual and emotional means are more frequent and the abuse of authority under the veil of business, social or emotional ties is certainly more common.

Masochism represents the reverse with sexual satisfaction derived from the experience of pain or suffering. It is commonly accepted as a characteristic seen more frequently in women but not unknown in men. Here the same combination between aggression and libido is said to exist but is directed inwards. Woman, with her passive biological and social rôle, lends herself by her receptivity to this mode of sexuality. In practice it is socially a less disturbing problem but the individual who relies exclusively on this method can easily become the unhappy victim of her needs, progressively unable to meet her increasing requirements for suffering humiliation.

A proper understanding of sado-masochistic mechanisms is of paramount importance to Christianity, a way of life inspired by the Cross and sacrifice. Suffering is one of the essential means for personal sanctification, and virginity or the single state dedicated to God a hallowed state. It is not surprising that when these ideals are ill-digested and sublimation incomplete or unsuccessful, some aspirants will become a prey to pathological outlets. While the individual sufferer must always be the object of our help, sympathy and compassion, it is particularly galling and a disservice to Christianity when sadism or masochism are misinterpreted as substitutes for genuine Christian virtues.

FRIGIDITY

This is a not uncommon difficulty for which psychiatric help is sought by the wife or her disappointed spouse. The complaint is a relative or absolute inability to enjoy sexual relations and the term is applied exclusively to a disability of the woman. Kinsey, who confined his study to actual orgasm, found that after twenty years of marriage eleven per cent of his sample had not experienced an orgasm. He also found that successful physical relations before marriage were correlated highly with success later on in marriage.

It has been generally assumed, and many authors have spent a good deal of time writing on the subject, that the success of the physical side of marriage depends on a wide knowledge of various techniques and their application by the husband. This is yet another fallacy based on the current philosophies which view man as a physical automaton bolstered up by the success of his conditioned reflexes. This wave of unfettered hedonism is passing and we are recognizing that frigidity is the result of more than one factor. Certainly the drive and approach of the man is important but so is the response of the woman. It is difficult to measure, but undoubtedly true, that there is a wide range in physical arousal and there are upper and lower limits beyond which any one organism will not respond. There are also a host of psychological and social determinants which must not be minimized. The girl's upbringing and the values she has received from her parents and educators on sex will be of paramount importance. So will the stability and happiness of her own home. At a deeper level, analytical writers will trace the source of the difficulty to the oedipal conflict, the incestuous desires remaining unresolved with exaggerated guilt feelings which censure adequate fulfilment. The "male protest" is another phrase coined to suggest that in woman there is the possibility of a revolt against men and her status and this may emerge, among other ways, as frigidity. In this way she is denying her feminine rôle. If to all this is added the distinctive reserve and suspicions which some parents inculcate in their daughters on sex, we have many ingredients from which to seek an explanation. Every one of these issues must be examined and the appropriate ones explored and if possible remedied. But success is hard to come by and much patience and perseverance is required. As a preventive measure, Kinsey points to the high correlation between premarital and post-marital success, but, even if this is a causal relationship, which he doubts, it is a source unacceptable to the Christian conscience and unlikely to find favour with Christians or anyone else. Frigidity is not infrequently associated with other neurotic features such as anxiety and tension and is a frequent accompaniment of depressive illness. Psychiatric help in these complicated occasions will prove of undoubted assistance.

IMPOTENCE

Impotence is an exclusively male disability characterized by the inability to perform the act of copulation. It is not as common as frigidity, occurring in less than one per cent of men under thirty-five. It is a natural accompaniment of ageing, but in elderly people it does not usually present psychiatric difficulties since it coincides with a diminution of sexual desire. In the first half of life, however, it presents acute problems especially after marriage has been contracted. Rarely is it a permanent condition; much more often it is only temporary. When the condition has been found to be permanent and antecedent to marriage, it provides the grounds for a dissolution of the bonds of matrimony.

There are some physical causes to account for this complaint but the majority of cases fall within the sphere of psychological disturbances. The wide range of sexual capacity, differences in upbringing, childhood experiences and attitudes to the opposite sex undoubtedly shape and contribute to the ultimate capacity of achieving the male biological rôle. Special circumstances such as an unsatisfactory mother–son relationship, which has engendered either excessive dependence on her or much hostility, may be displaced to the future wife with whom the same emotional difficulties will be experienced. The absence of a father may make the adoption of a similar rôle harder. Anxiety is commonly associated with this complaint and the vicious circle of attempt, failure, guilt and despondency producing more anxiety is seen frequently. Some success can be obtained by timely intervention and the successful interruption of this circle. Although, understandably enough, attention is concentrated on the man, the personality, needs and demands of the wife are paramount. If her requirements are clearly in excess of what is possible, some modification on her part is essential. This is obvious in the men who, while unsuccessful with their wives, are successful with others. Such cases present a grave temptation to the psychiatrist who is attempting to bolster up the confidence of his patient by encouraging any and all occasions of successful attempts. The limitation of such an approach, moral issues apart, is the encouragement of a course which does little to evaluate basic conflicts, confirms immature habits and adds the anxiety of immoral behaviour. Impotence, as with the rest of sexual difficulties, is not uncommonly associated with personality and neurotic disabilities, the treatment of which may indirectly help this symptom. As in the case of frigidity, loss of sexual desire and capacity to perform are often features of a depressive illness which will improve as the depression lifts. Homosexuals may marry as a means of reassuring themselves of the normality of their sexual inclinations. When the result is a failure, the ingredients of tragedy are present both for the wife, who entered a contract of deception, and for the husband, who is confirmed in his despair.

MARRIAGE AND PSYCHIATRY

The part which psychiatry can play in the achievement of successful marriages is ill-defined. There are those who are swept away by the tempting but unsubstantiated analytic tenets. In their opinion, the successful preparation and consummation of marriage depend on the strict adherence to the enlightened avoidance of man's self-inflicted prohibitions and inhibitions. Others will shun any direct professional responsibility for a contract which is seen completely as a social and spiritual event well outside their competence as doctors. The majority subscribe to a midway course. If this is adopted, what can the psychiatrist offer?

To begin with, enough studies have established the fact that the incidence of mental disease is much higher in the single than in the married.[9] The reason for this may be a matter of selection—the potentially unstable person does not enter into marriage—or, alternatively, the married state exerts certain beneficial effects. At present we have few available facts to settle this issue and much research is required. The psychological facts operating are of profound interest to the Christian, who is not a disinterested observer, having placed traditionally so much emphasis on the rôle of the single life dedicated to God.

Before marriage, the physician can offer advice based on his knowledge of the genetics of psychiatric disease. The dangers of inheritance, the risks of cousin marriages can be pointed out, while frequently reassurance can be given to those who have no grounds for worry. A much greater difficulty is the assessment of the value of this state as a cure for neurotic disorders. Generally speaking, the advice will be against this form of therapy. Even more important is the task of acquainting spiritual advisers with the dangers of advocating this way out for sexual difficulties, which are part and

[9] Odegard Ormulu, "Marriage and Mental Disease", *Journal of Mental Science* (1946), xcviii, p. 35.

parcel of a neurotic constellation, the sexual side of which is but one symptom of the disorder.

Usually help will be sought after marriage. Some of the difficulties will be the expression of psychotic disorder. The general loss of interest in the depressed will interfere with the attention given to home, family and sex and, if this is misinterpreted, misunderstandings follow. The suspicions and jealousies of the paranoid schizophrenic directed towards the spouse are particularly painful experiences when the cause is unknown. The financial irresponsibilities and sexual excesses of the hypomanic spouse need explanation.

The bulk of the work will undoubtedly come from disorders of personality and neurotic disabilities. There is no other state so ideally designed to bring forth the inadequacies of personality or to tax the deficiencies of the neurotic. Successful marriages are based on the mutual and freely exchanged gifts of adult and supplementing personalities. The immaturity, dependency and limitations of the histrionic, paranoid and inadequate personalities and the presence of neurotic mechanisms of adaptation lead on to discord, recriminations and unhappiness. These are the types of problems which some psychiatrics feel lie outside their province. Certainly the results of therapy are disappointing. This is not surprising since what is usually required is a radical modification of a way of life. To accomplish anything useful, patience, fortitude and the ability to give up childish needs and immediate satisfaction for the adult postponement of gratification are required. The ability to give and to suffer, to acknowledge and measure up to one's emotional requirements are also important. These are difficult goals, wholly attainable in a few; partial modification is the best that can be hoped for in the rest. But for Christians in general and Catholics in particular, who accept the indissolubility of marriage, an effort must be made to help and, provided there is an element of goodwill and a sincere desire to overcome the difficulties, the outlook is not hopeless. If cures are the exception, sufficient adjustment to make life tolerable is not impossible.

Sexual difficulties are invariably prominent and, while each case has to be assessed on its own merits, the informed Christian psychiatrist can achieve a great deal by clarifying moral from social transgression. There has grown up a folklore, which passes as Christian sexual ethics, which is no more than a conglomeration of inflated fallacies. The valid expression of physical love in its manifold manifestations is suffocated by irrelevant prohibitions. Chastity, which is part of the virtue of temperance, is confused with Manicheism and the essence of self-control distorted. Hostility towards the spouse and indirectly towards the Church can spring from such falsification. The sacramental life and the practice of faith are sometimes abandoned. When some of these points are disentangled, not only are conjugal relations improved but the spiritual life is reinvigorated. If the doctor has the well-being of the whole human nature, both spiritual and physical, at heart, the management of such cases provides a fruitful source for the accomplishment of truly valuable and apostolic work.

Advice on the use of the infertile period, in justified circumstances, will lift the anxiety against another immediate pregnancy. Since 1951, when Pius XII[10] made it absolutely clear that the safe period can be used temporarily or permanently for medical reasons, patients with psychiatric conditions which warrant such precautions can be advised accordingly. Schizophrenics, unable to look after further children, sufferers from Huntingdon's Chorea, an extremely rare, incurable, dementing illness are two examples for the permanent use of the infertile period, while many others will qualify for a shorter period. The use of the infertile period will largely apply to Catholics. The author is aware of the controversies that surround the subject and the differences of

[10] Pius XII, *Acta Apostolicae Sedis* (1951), XVIII, p. 835. (English translation, *The Clergy Review* (1951), XXXVI, p. 379.)

approach amongst the Christian denominations. However, this theme is outside the scope of this book. It is sufficient to point out that the advocacy of methods inconsistent with the dictates of a patient's conscience can do little else than add guilt and anxiety. The Catholic Marriage Advisory Council offers nation-wide facilities to meet the particular issues affecting Catholics in Great Britain.

CHAPTER VI

ALCOHOLISM

And the third day there was a marriage in Cana of Galilee; and the mother of Jesus was there. And Jesus also was invited and his disciples to the marriage. And the wine failing the mother of Jesus saith to him: They have no wine. And Jesus saith to her: Woman, what is that to me and to thee? My hour is not yet come. His mother saith to the waiters: Whatsoever he say to you, do ye. Now there were set there six water-pots of stone, according to the manner of purifying of the Jews, containing two or three measures apiece. Jesus saith to them: Fill the water-pots with water. And they filled them up to the brim. And Jesus saith to them: Draw out now and carry to the chief steward of the feast. And they carried it. And when the chief steward had tasted the water made wine and knew not whence it was, but the waiters knew who had drawn the water, the chief steward calleth the bridegroom and saith to him: Every man at first setteth forth good wine and when men have well drunk, then that which is worse; but thou has kept the good wine until now. This beginning of miracles did Jesus in Cana of Galilee and manifested his glory (John 2. 1–11, Douay).

The view of the Catholic Church and the majority of the Christian denominations is that the taking of alcohol in moderation is not sinful. Morally, and in view of our Lord's first recorded miracle, it is not tenable to maintain, as some do, that alcohol is an evil and its consumption innately wrong. This would be equally incompatible with events at the Last Supper and the use of wine at the altar for the Eucharist. Moving from these sacred uses, Western societies have long established traditions sanctioning the use of alcoholic drinks on festive and other occasions, always drawing the line between consumption justified by the social and personal requirements of the occasion and excess for its own sake. Drinking on a small scale is in fact extremely common. For the majority, this is a perfectly safe type of recreation, but there are solid minorities, varying in numbers from country to country, who become alcoholics. Alcoholism is defined in the present context as causing damage to the individual or society or both.[1] It is not easy to get accurate figures for the incidence of alcoholism. Dr Jellinek, a world authority on this subject, has calculated that, of fifty million Americans who drink alcohol in some form, the total of excessive drinkers is three million of whom 750,000 become chronic alcoholic addicts.[2] The proportion of men to women affected in the U.S.A. is six to one. The incidence in Great Britain is not so high but a sizeable problem remains and there are also more men than women addicts although the ratio has dropped to two to one.

Society's attitude to the alcoholic varies considerably. He can be ostracized as a wicked person, treated with contempt or pitied for the weakness of his will, sympathized with but nonetheless held responsible. To these traditional views, there has emerged in the last twenty-five years an entirely new approach. It is that alcoholism is a disease, should be approached as such and removed from the arena of moral responsibility. This view has been adopted extensively in the United States but has not infiltrated public opinion to the same extent in Great Britain although British physicians handling alcoholics have largely been won over to this concept. One of the reasons for reorientating the approach to alcoholism is the growing understanding that it is not a unitary concept, that in fact there are different types of alcoholism. Five main types have been recently described.[3]

[1] E. M. Jellinek, *The Disease Concept of Alcoholism* (1960), p. 35.
[2] *Idem, Alcohol, Science and Society*, New Haven, Conn. (1945), pp. 23 ff.
[3] *Idem, The Disease Concept of Alcoholism*, New Haven, Conn. (1960), pp. 36 ff.

The first one represents undisciplined drinking to relieve psychological or physical discomfort. It is heavy, continuous, has severe adverse effects financially and is detrimental to the social and family stability of the individual but there is no loss of control or inability to abstain for long or short periods or to terminate the drinking. The second variety depends on social customs, that is the person lives in a milieu, such as a wine-producing area, or works in a firm that produces alcoholic drinks, where he drinks heavily. There are no psychological or physical reasons but inevitably severe physical damage is sustained and of course the family suffers financially. The third and fourth varieties are distinguished by the fact that loss of control is exhibited, added to which there is now craving and physical dependence on the drink. They are distinguished by a simple criterion. The third variety will allow interruption of drinking for a day or two, the loss of control operating in the amount taken on any one occasion. The fourth variety will not permit cessation even for a day, but control is exhibited over the amount consumed on each occasion. The fifth type is called periodic alcoholism, in which people drink excessively and potentially with much harm but the bouts are irregular and control is not lost for the period in between.

A good deal of emphasis is placed on the words control and physical dependence. When a person reaches the stage when he is unable by any voluntary means to control his drinking, and if, in these circumstances, he suffers dire physical symptoms when alcohol is not available (including collapse and death), then a true addiction has set in, in no way different from other medical states due to drugs of addiction. At this stage, there is no question of dealing with a free agent; disease is present and the person must be treated as sick. The large majority of alcoholics belong to the third category and we can next inquire into some of the reasons for this.

There are a very few unfortunate people who become addicts from the very first drink they take. A closer examination reveals a mixture of severely disturbed personalities who have found, by accident or design, one form of compensation for their inadequacies. Next in line are those psychotically disturbed; the schizophrenic, gradually slipping away from unsatisfactory emotional contacts with his fellow human beings, takes to alcohol; the depressed will seek comfort for his abnormal and excessive sadness; the hypomanic wants to express in a concrete manner his high spirits and general jubilation. Attention in all these groups must be primarily directed to the underlying disease process. Alcoholism in these cases is only a symptom of a disintegrating personality. Mention has been made in the first variety described of a type of alcoholism which is brought about by psychological factors which do not lead to loss of control and addiction. Leading psychogenic factors in this group are anxiety and inability to deal with everyday tensions and conflicts. Everyone knows the calming effects of a drink in a stressful situation. When the underlying state makes such stresses and strains a permanent feature of a personality, then alcoholism of the first variety ensues but sometimes it progresses to the third type with loss of control and physical dependence develops.

So far certain psychological explanations have been outlined for the eventual development of addiction. The ranks of addicts are filled from various sources. To these belong business men who have to conduct business in a context of social engagements at which heavy drinking features prominently; cheerful, easy-going persons who entertain and are entertained frequently with social prestige attached to the quantity and quality of the liquor available; promoters and salesmen in the alcoholic trade. A very high proportion of addicts can trace the origin of their alcoholism to these backgrounds. Finally, periodic drinkers may be driven to it by such recurrent disorders as epilepsy or swings in mood which, while not severe enough to be recognized as frank depression or elation, may disturb the rhythm of life sufficiently to account for the excessive drinking.

While psychological and social factors go a long way to provide satisfactory reasons for the initiation of drinking habits, they are clearly not the sole explanation. Many people are subject to similar stresses and do not succumb to this disease. A great deal of work, at the present moment only suggestive, points to the presence of inherited, genetic factors which increase the vulnerability of the victims and would offer a more satisfactory explanation.

The disease concept of alcoholism must inevitably have some impact on the moral evaluation of the alcoholic. After the above brief outline, it would no longer be consistent to lump alcoholics together and to point a common finger of responsibility at all of them. Some, the psychotics for instance, would be in no way responsible and the neurotic and those suffering from personality disorders would be responsible to the degree that their freedom of action has not been impaired by the psychiatric disorder. But what of those who do not belong to these categories? Clearly, in such cases, these individuals can foresee and assess the sinful nature of their excesses and, in theory at least, should be able to take steps to avoid repetition.

Writing on this issue Fr John Ford, S.J., writes: "Objectively (such) alcoholics are responsible for their condition.... But subjectively it seems to me, not many are mortally guilty.... Very few foresee addiction.... Very few believe they will ever become drunks. They succeed in deceiving themselves." This ability to deceive themselves and others is one of the keys to the transition from sobriety to alcoholism. Whatever the initial grounds for this disorder, its development to the final stages of addiction, which may take anything from three to twenty years, takes a recognized and progressive course. Initially bouts of excessive drinking are rare and a satisfactory explanation is offered for each one. After a few years, these bouts increase in number and they may now be accompanied by amnesic features. There is no recollection of the drunken evening and even a denial. Dependence increases and the drinking may become secretive. The time-table is rearranged, and there is some drinking in the morning besides the excess of the evening. There is an air of increased superficial confidence with repeated denials that the subject is on the way to alcoholism. To prove this, he goes for short periods "on the water wagon", abstaining. These periods are brief but essential for the reassurance of the victim. The family begin to suffer financially and socially as funds are directed to the bottle and friends begin to drop off. The final stages are approached when there is drinking round the clock. Hope has now vanished and the alcoholic is bent on getting the last possible ounce of contentment from his drink. Hypocrisy is lost and outright callousness and indifference overtake the subject. Husband-wife relations are strained, frequently as a result of repeated accusations on the part of the husband, whose failing sexual capacities are coupled with morbid jealousies of imaginary lovers entertained by his wife. Gainful employment may come to an end and the abjection be completed by the sale of personal valuables or those of the spouse in a last desperate effort to obtain drink. Delirium tremens, physical exhaustion and other pathologies complete the picture of a pathetic figure who has in the last stages abandoned God, family and friends for alcohol.

By this stage, admission to hospital is essential. Treatment outside is hopeless and doomed to failure. Therapy will in all cases mean the building up of the debilitated body and, by stages or abruptly, the cessation of alcohol consumption. The next stage, building up and maintaining an aversion to drinking, is not so easily accomplished. A prolonged period in hospital, even up to a year, may be necessary. Psychotherapy alone or in combination with other techniques has been tried. Another approach is to associate drinking with an unpleasant experience or to decondition the bad habit. This can be done by ingesting alcohol and at the same time receiving an injection which will lead to nausea and vomiting of the alcohol within a short period. If this combination is sustained long enough, the patient gradually begins to hate the sight of the bottle. Another treatment commonly in use at present is a drug which is taken daily by mouth. If no alcohol is taken no ill feeling is experienced but, if an alcoholic drink is imbibed after the drug, the combination produces unpleasant feelings of thumping in the head, nausea, sweating and generally intense discomfort. This is a very successful treatment but it depends on the willingness of the subject to go on taking the tablet regularly after leaving hospital. Alcoholics can relapse years later and vigilance must not waver even after a prolonged period of successful abstinence.

If an alcoholic ceases drinking there is a void in his life, a void which needs to be filled. He may have to re-enter the community bereft of friends and status. His drinking connections are now taboo and time hangs heavily. There must be some sort of outlet and support in this new way of life. This need is filled with outstanding success by the association known as "Alcoholics Anonymous", a body composed of former alcoholics. Once a person has joined the A.A., he is assured of an extensive network of assistance and support. He will be accepted in other members' houses, receive prompt help at any time if he encounters or anticipates a period of temptation and generally he will find a society where he matters as a person and his former alcoholism is a sign of his present strength and conversion. This is a plan which is not built on platitudes but on certain affirmative attitudes developed in 12 steps.

1. We admitted that we were powerless over alcohol—that our lives had become unmanageable.
2. Came to believe that a Power greater than ourselves could restore us to sanity.
3. Made a decision to turn our will and our lives over to the care of God *as we understood him.*
4. Made a searching and fearless moral inventory of ourselves.

5. Admitted to God, to ourselves, and to another human being the exact nature of our wrongs.

6. Were entirely ready to have God remove all these defects of character.

7. Humbly asked him to remove our shortcomings.

8. Made a list of all persons we had harmed and became willing to make amends to them all.

9. Made direct amends to such people wherever possible, except when to do so would injure them or others.

10. Continued to take personal inventory, and when we were wrong, promptly admitted it.

11. Sought through prayer and meditation to improve our conscious contact with God *as we understood him*, praying only for knowledge of his will for us and the power to carry that out.

12. Having had a spiritual awakening as a result of these steps, we tried to carry this message to alcoholics and to practise these principles in all our affairs.

The religious character of the association is quite clear and the flexibility of its approach as shown in steps 3 and 11 makes it perfectly acceptable to Catholics, Protestants and other denominations. Each is free to pursue his renewed spiritual life in accordance with his own faith and tradition. The considerable success of A.A. is not in the least surprising to any Christian, who sees the submission of the human will to the divine plan as the ennobling enhancement of his life on earth and the means of fulfilling his eternal destiny. Furthermore, any organization which utilizes individual and collective energy to love and support mutual members fulfils perfectly the Christian ideal of human relations.

This chapter has tried to summarize a currently developing concept of alcoholism as a disease process of many varieties springing from different backgrounds. Such an approach facilitates the evaluation of alcoholism in general, modifies traditional views on the uniformity of its wickedness and paves the way for more constructive, realistic and preventive measures.

CHAPTER VII

THERAPEUTIC METHODS

The treatment of mental disorder divides itself into two distinct and different methods. The first consists of physical treatments, among which are electro-convulsive and deep or modified insulin therapy, narcosis, leucotomy and recently the introduction of a wide variety of drugs. The second is covered under the broad term of psychotherapy, the essence of which is a verbal dialogue between the patient and doctor. Psychotherapy includes an analysis, the use of analytically orientated methods to achieve limited goals in a shorter period, group psychotherapy and counselling, which implies reassurance and advice. The choice of therapy will depend on the type of disorder and the outlook and background of the doctor. In the U.S.A., for example, there is a widespread use of analysis and psychotherapy, while in Great Britain the physical methods are used more extensively. Except for a few conditions, such as electro-convulsive therapy for depressive illness, there is little evidence to indicate absolutely the course to be adopted. This is a difficulty which does not confront psychiatry alone and it is to be expected that further information will delineate the appropriate measures more clearly as it has done in other branches of medicine. From the moral point of view, interest has concentrated on the psychotherapeutic approaches. Here, whatever particular brand of therapy may be in use, all schools trace their origin to Freud's concepts. Invariably these are tinged with his views on sex, responsibility, morality, man's aspirations, his freedom and the aims of human nature. A great deal has been written on all these issues and the interested reader is referred to some of these works at the end of the chapter. Here we can do no more than outline some of the main points.

PSYCHOANALYSIS

Up to Freud's time, neurotics were treated with hypnosis, suggestion and physical techniques such as baths and electrotherapy. He concentrated on the talking therapy, itself not new, but the technique of psychoanalysis is entirely his original contribution. Impressed by the importance of the unconscious, he devised a way of making this part of man accessible to himself. He placed the patient on a couch, requiring him to talk about everything and anything; no subject was barred because of its content, moral or social depravity or unpleasantness. This was described as free association. The patient was thus able to reach his unconscious and bring forth emotional experiences long since repressed which were nonetheless active. Dreams were also used which, in Freud's view, were expressions of wish fulfilment heavily cloaked in the strange symbolism of the dream material. Because the content to be expressed was unacceptable in any other form, it had to be hidden in various symbols and the dream, hitherto a mass of mysterious happenings, began to have meaning, reinforcing the information that was coming from the free association revelations. This first phase of the analysis takes on the nature of a confession or abreaction of highly charged material, conscious and unconscious. It soon became evident that this alone was not sufficient and the analysis entered into the second phase called transference. Here the patient identifies his analyst with one of the parental figures and forms a deep enough relationship so as to be able to relive his emotional experiences with his doctor who now represents father or mother. Hostility hitherto felt, but without the ability to express it, a submissive or an aggressive attitude, any form of deep emotional feeling are expressed and experienced towards the analyst. This necessitates re-living in a way those early emotional experiences which have led to the current neurotic practices. Finally, the analysis concludes with the successful resolution of the transference. The patient has gained insight into his principal conflicts, neurotic methods of dealing with them and, by reliving his feelings and emotions, has successfully outgrown his patho-logical habits and asserts his integrated independence of both parents and analyst. During the analysis, the analyst's rôle is to remain a passive receiver of all the patient gives him. He passes no judgement, neither encourages nor dis-courages, decries nor sets an example. He is an intensely interested participant, whose weapons are silence and inter-pretation. At the appropriate moment he helps the patient by pointing out or suggesting the possible significance and reason for a course of action, feeling or experience. His object throughout is to help the patient to gain insight into the meaning of the pattern of life he is unfolding, to indicate where neurotic behaviour is covering up emotional conflicts and to bring the patient to the point of truly evaluating his motives. Lifelong neurotic defences dissipating energy are uncovered and dealt with.

An analysis demands from three to five weekly sessions of approximately an hour for a period of three to five years with an analyst, who is usually a trained psychiatrist but can be a lay person. The analyst must have had a training analysis prior to commencing this type of work. This is to prevent his own unconscious conflicts from interfering with the therapy as well as to give him a practical experience of what he is going to undertake in the future.

Freudian analysis relies mainly on uncovering unconscious conflicts. When this is done, it is considered that the analysis is complete or as near complete as possible. Emphasis is placed on reaching events in the past which have contributed to the present and, in technical terms, this is wholly a re-ductive process. Adler stressed the importance of the present circumstances and Jung aims at a synthesis of the past and the present into a personal transformation and rejuvenation for the future. There are details of addition, subtraction and emphasis which each school has developed independently but none contradict fundamentally this broad picture.

If psychoanalysis is accepted as an additional weapon in the treatment of mental illness, and this has by no means received universal approval, then there are certain poignant issues relative to Christianity. It has been seen that the analyst remains neutral as at times undoubted immoral practices are unfolded. It should be noted that he remains neutral, not that he encourages such acts. This would be totally out of keeping with analytic procedure. The critics will go on to point out further that it is impossible to disregard Freud's view that religion was an illusion and that its activities were no more than substitutes for libidinal energy. If God had no place in his philosophy, this could hardly be kept out of his approach to treatment.

These serious charges need answers. To begin with, it is reasonable to hold that the material with which the analyst and the patient are primarily concerned is the irrational, unacknowledged compulsive content of the unconscious, which has a bearing on present conscious conduct. Because of its very character, it lies beyond the formal hold and responsibility of the patient and the analyst does no more than accompany the patient on a journey that seeks such sources. If present immoral conduct is to have an opportunity of changing in these patients, this journey is essential and can be achieved with the help of the trained expert. Secondly, it is the primary aim of the analyst to give no advice. If he condemns any behaviour he joins the legion of others from the parents downwards who have done so without effecting a change. If he approves, he maintains the immature, childish and neurotic mechanisms which are the objects of therapy. In his neutral rôle, his sole objective is to render the patient capable of dealing with all his problems in an adult, mature and integrated way which means, of course, the moral way as well. Where the Christian analyst parts company with many of his colleagues who cannot agree with him, is when religion is ignored either as a psychological entity, part and parcel of the nature of man, or as a force conducive to psychological health. Jung has emphasized repeatedly the rôle of religion in the wholeness of man but other followers of Freud are beginning to reject the monopoly of the biological approach. Some exegetists of Freud have tried to work out formulas by which his philosophy and his therapeutic techniques are separated sufficiently not to interfere with the practical aspects of the treatment. It is difficult to see how this can be achieved unless some of the philosophical and theoretical tenets are rejected. This is the only way out for the Christian analyst who practises the Freudian method. In practice, this is not difficult and in no way interferes with the basic healing process.

Even when the indications are clear, an analysis is a long term undertaking, costly (each session costing between £3 and £5 in Great Britain or between $15 and $50 in the U.S.A.) and thus by necessity open to a few selected patients. More frequently, a shorter course of psychotherapy (six to twelve months) is attempted, aiming at some limited goals, indicated by the leading symptoms. The same principles operate whereby the patient is helped to gain insight and substitute healthy, productive and effective behaviour for neurotic and disabling symptoms. Its shorter duration necessitates a more active intervention on the part of the psychotherapist without any transgression, as far as possible, of the patient's freedom to act as an independent agent.

The growing demand for such psychotherapeutic procedures and the relative lack of qualified physicians to cope with them has prompted the search for means by which effective psychotherapy can be given simultaneously to a group of patients. Group psychotherapy is meeting this need. Five to ten patients with a similar range of problems meet together and are assisted by the doctor present to discuss their difficulties. The doctor does not play a prominent part, allowing the patients to unfold their feelings, to express, defend or when necessary curb their emotions under the social pressures of the group and progressively lose their sense of isolation. The group is the microcosm where they can act out their neurotic tendencies, discern the mutual distortions of normality and, to a varying degree, penetrate and overcome their shortcomings by the encouragement and support they can give each other.

While the doctor never ceases to aim at the eventual self-governing, self-directing independent person who is no longer in need of his help, it has to be admitted that there will be many patients who will never reach this stage and will need protracted support. They rely on the doctor and will go on pressing for directives on how to run their lives. It is very difficult in these circumstances to despatch the patient with a curt rejection. Ideals of therapy have to be modified, for beyond the scientific concept of disease and treatment lies suffering humanity whose alleviation must always be the primary aim of medicine. It is of course these patients who will tax to the utmost the gifts of the psychiatrist. When the resources of the text books are exhausted he will in the last resort turn to his own private experience. To offer what has proved successful in one's life implies a communication of an order of values that has moulded this life. The patients' dependence and level of confidence usually means that they frequently act on the advice given. It is a situation fraught with danger. Exaggerated fears are often heard in the Christian community that under these conditions the only advice likely to be given is a host of immoral directives appertaining to sex. While individual abuses undoubtedly occur, it can be safely generalized that the integrity of the majority of practising psychiatrists, whatever their beliefs, is beyond criticism. Even if they do not share an identical outlook with their Christian patients, they are unlikely to advise any conduct likely to clash with the dictates of the patient's conscience.

This does not mean that they or their Christian colleagues may not be compelled for a time to tolerate sinful conduct arising out of the patient's symptomatology. Toleration does not mean approval but is often a necessary, short or prolonged accompaniment. Pius XII in his allocution on psychotherapy and religion stated:

> Respect for God and his holiness must always be reflected in man's conscious acts. That is why what is called "material sin" (involuntary transgression of the law either through ignorance or impairment of the will) is something which should not exist, and which constitutes in the moral order a reality which is not indifferent. From this a conclusion follows for psychotherapy. In the presence of material sin it cannot remain neutral. It can, for the moment, tolerate what remains inevitable. But it must know that God cannot justify such an action. With still less reason can psychotherapy counsel a patient to commit material sin on the ground that it will be without subjective (responsible) guilt. One may never counsel a conscious action which would be a deformation and not an image of the divine perfection.

There are some superficial similarities between an analysis and analytically orientated psychotherapy on the one hand and the sacrament of confession on the other. There are those who express exaggerated views in both directions, believing that all psychotherapy is superfluous if only attention is paid to the life of the spirit, including frequent confession, and, at the other extreme, that the priest's duties have been replaced by those of the psychotherapist. To settle this controversy all that is required is a closer examination of the two activities.

Confession, as practised in the Catholic Church, is accepted as a sacrament, that is, an instrument of grace, an external sign to indicate the inward flow of the supernatural love, friendship and strength of God to man. Here the penitent acknowledges his sins and confesses them to a priest. This is a rational, deliberate act which deals with conscious transgressions. The subject matter of the patient in analysis is, as we have indicated, the irrational subconscious and unconscious material which is interfering with the normal functioning of his life. The content of a confession is divided in theological terms into remote and proximate matter and form. The remote matter indicates the sins to be confessed, the proximate the confession, contrition and satisfaction, and the form is the words of forgiveness pronounced by the priest after he has pronounced judgement on what he has heard. But, above all, he is the means by which grace has flowed into the soul of the penitent. The psychotherapist in this sense gives little and certainly is not responsible for grace, he passes no judgement and the patient is under no obligation to confess anything. Fr White points out in *God and the Unconscious*[1] that the evil which the penitent confesses is the *malum culpae* or the evil which he has done, but the evil of neurotic illness, the exchange between therapist and patient, is the *malum poenae* or misfortune which men suffer. Faith, St Thomas tells us, is the humble receptivity of the human mind to the Unseen and the Unknown[2] and in the sacrament of penance, the faithful are engaged in a personal enrichment from this divine source. The analyst also deals with things unseen and unknown, man's unconscious shadow. He is busy unfettering the shackles which may impede the journey to the Unseen and the Unknown.

PHYSICAL METHODS

Electro-Convulsive Therapy

This treatment consists of passing a brief electric impulse through the brain while the patient is unconscious. The whole procedure is over in a matter of minutes; it is extremely safe and efficacious in certain types of illnesses. The patient re-

[1] Victor White, *God and the Unconscious*, Fontana Books, London (1960), p. 181.

[2] *Summa Theologica*, IIa–IIae, 2 and 3.

ceives what in practice amounts to an epileptic convulsion. Exactly how it works is not known but the end results amply justify this empirical procedure. Its main place in psychiatric therapy is in the treatment of affective illness, in particular depression. Before its introduction all the misery of this condition could continue on an average for six to nine months. A successful course of six to nine shocks spread over two to three weeks can cut the duration of the illness to a matter of a few weeks. The only unpleasant side effect is a temporary impairment of memory which usually lasts no more than a month to six weeks. There are no moral contra-indications to this treatment.

Insulin Therapy

One of the many substances for the normal functioning of the brain is sugar. This can be reduced drastically by means of insulin in the circulating blood which supplies the brain. The aim is to reach a level of unconsciousness which is maintained for about thirty minutes. An expert team is in attendance and about thirty comas are given over a period of two to three months. Schizophrenic illness in its early stages is the sole recipient of this treatment and up to recently it has had an extensive vogue. Doubts are now being cast on its usefulness and with the emergence of powerful drugs it will recede into the background. Once again there are no moral contra-indications.

Chemotherapy

The types of drug which the psychiatrist uses are designed to combat the common and recurrent complaints of tension, anxiety, restlessness, irritation and variation in mood, particularly that of depression. The barbiturates and the bromides were the stock agents but recently giant strides have been made in this field. Tranquillizers, antidepressant drugs and new powerful ones designed to tackle psychotic manifestations are now part of the therapeutic armoury.

During the war, the barbiturates were used to produce continuous periods of deep sleep or even stupor. They were effective in cases of acute anxiety attacks or panic. In peacetime, these applications are limited. Drugs can be used to help a very tense person to speak about an emotionally charged experience when it is causing him so much anxiety that he is unable either to remember or to recapitulate it under ordinary conditions. Under these circumstances, provided the patient has given his consent, these agents can be used to reduce his conscious inhibition and, in the consequent drowsy state, enable him to recapture and relive the painful incidents. Needless to say, here as elsewhere, the doctor is the recipient of information which he must respect with professional secrecy, withholding its revelation when important, except in special circumstances.

Leucotomy

This is an operation which cuts one of the nerve connections between one part of the brain, the frontal lobe, and another centre, the thalamus. It has been found empirically that this surgical procedure offers considerable relief in certain psychiatric disorders characterized chiefly by agitation, tension, excessive restlessness and worry. This relief is obtained at the expense of some personality changes such as indifference to events and people, with some weakening of foresight and judgement and, in some cases, unconcern for long-established social and moral habits. In the early stages, excessive zeal and enthusiasm produced some end results in which these side effects were severe and the range of human freedom and ability to exercise the will grievously handicapped. Such an outcome, combined with the essential character of the operation, which is the destruction of healthy tissue, gave rise to considerable anxiety regarding the legitimacy of such a procedure. The principle here, as in all surgical therapy, rests on the justification of sacrificing a part, healthy or diseased, if the well-being of the whole is thereby preserved.

To remove or destroy healthy tissue must obviously have a proportionately graver reason than the removal of a diseased part which threatens the integrity of the rest. In the case of leucotomy, certain conditions must exist before the operation can be justified morally. Firstly, all efficacious treatment, including the new means of drug therapy, should have been tried. Secondly, when all these treatments have failed, there must exist a severe and incapacitating residual state. Finally, every effort must be made to minimize any harmful damage to the personality. In practice all these conditions are fulfilled before the operation is undertaken. Recently, fewer patients have been subjected to it because the new drugs have helped to control symptoms which were indications for the operations. Modifications and improvements in the actual operation and more judicious selection of patients have all combined to reduce the undesirable complications.

De-conditioning

Neurotic symptoms are explained by the Pavlovian theory simply on the basis of the foundation of maladaptive conditioned habits. The logical treatment therefore is the deconditioning of such behaviour and the learning of a more appropriate one in its place. This can be illustrated by the following example. A patient may have a phobia which prevents him from entering a crowded place such as a cinema, a church, a bus or a subway. Every time he approaches one of these locations he experiences a severe attack of anxiety, which is incapacitating and prevents further progress toward the desired spot. Therapy commences and has as its first goal the extinction of the anxiety. This is accomplished by getting the patient to approach, in the company of his instructor, progressively nearer, the cinema for example, without experiencing anxiety. The first time he can go no nearer than a furlong away. In the course of a number of attempts, he gets right up to the cinema without experiencing anxiety. This is first done in the presence of the instructor and then in his absence. The next phase is to acquire the desired goal and the procedure is repeated entering the cinema, again by stages. Finally, all anxiety is lost and the person can go to the cinema unattended and without suffering.

These methods have recently gained a good deal of publicity. They make an appeal by their simplicity, the speed with which success is attained and the total avoidance of any resort to unconscious motives. They are certainly occasionally extremely impressive but closer examination has not substantiated some of the exaggerated claims. Furthermore, they are not without moral implications. If the behaviour desired is in the sexual field, as for example the treatment of impotence, some accounts have not hesitated to advise the progressive utilization of persons outside the marriage bond in order to gain the desired experience. In the vast majority of cases such contra-indications do not exist and treatment can be undertaken, if its value is confirmed, and in the presence of justifying circumstances.

Hypnosis

In hypnosis the subject consciously and deliberately withdraws his attention from all outside phenomena and concentrates entirely on the person who is the hypnotizing agent. The subject is aware only of his own inner world and his only contact with the environment is through the hypnotist. Gradually a sleep-like state is achieved which can become a profound trance. During it, the patient can recollect experiences forgotten for a long time and, indeed, episodes going back to his childhood. The most impressive feature of this trance-state is the suggestibility of the subject. He will perform the most complicated activities at the command of his hypnotist and experience the most exotic hallucinations through suggestion. The medical importance of this lies in the fact that the subject may be given beneficial suggestions with regard to his health. For example, an asthmatic may be told that during the next week he will have no asthmatic attacks.

After awakening he will not remember this instruction but true enough he will be free from asthma for the following week. Hypnosis has limited but real application in psychiatry with such problems as anxiety, neurotic symptoms, psychosomatic disorders, alcoholism and other forms of addiction. It should be practised with caution and by the expert. It is certainly no panacea but neither is it a "quack" practice.

The hypnotic trance has certain moral implications which should be outlined. The deliberate acceptance of any diminution of man's freedom and the operation of his free will, however temporary, should only be undertaken for adequate reasons. In an operation, for example, anaesthesia temporarily removes all such potentiality but it is nevertheless a permissible action for obvious reasons of health. In hypnosis, the loss is not comparable but equally good indications should be present for its usage; medical ones, such as therapy or properly conducted research, would fulfil these criteria. Another issue appertains to the possibility of behaving or carrying out instructions contrary to one's ethical and moral standards. While these fears are justified in theory, extensive experience indicates that very little can be accomplished by the hypnotist without the express agreement and consent of the subject. The whole success of the procedure depends on the voluntary cooperation of the person being hypnotized. There are examples in the literature indicating that, when a hypnotist tries to make the subject carry out instructions contrary to the latter's deep convictions, there is increasing resistance which ultimately ends in refusal.

Castration

Sterilization of the male by removal of the testes has been advocated for such conditions as psychopathy, in which sexual misconduct is the leading symptom, homosexuality and exhibitionism. It is a rare form of therapy on the Continent but is not practised in Great Britain. In general medicine, such a sterilization would be lawful both in men and women where it has been shown that, for example, a cancer is being activated by the products of the sexual organs. In this instance these organs would be acting in a malignant capacity and directly influencing a disease process adversely. There is no satisfactory evidence at present to link causally any of these psychiatric conditions with the hormonal secretion of these glands and in these circumstances it is difficult to see how castration can be a justifiable procedure.

CHAPTER VIII

CHILD PSYCHIATRY

Perhaps of all the specialities within psychological medicine that of child psychiatry is the one most misunderstood. This is understandable because of its comparatively late arrival and incorporation into the main body of psychiatric thought. It has also received the sort of publicity that least expresses its fundamental work while managing to capture unwelcome attention. It would be perhaps a slight exaggeration, but not too wide of the mark, to suggest that the laymen interprets child psychiatry as those precepts which instruct parents and educators to keep their hands off the children and put the blame for every disorder squarely on the shoulders of anyone except the child. This in turn has provoked angry retorts from all those responsible for the care of children, much energy being thus dissipated in an exchange of mutual recriminations and misunderstanding. What is more, instead of accepting the child psychiatric clinic as a source of help and advice, far too often the thought of being seen there is interpreted by parents as a judgement and sentence in advance for some failure of upbringing. For Christian parents and educators, zealous of their rights and conscious of long-established tradition, child psychiatry is another unwelcome intrusion from sources which have yet to prove their worth and stand the test of time.

Undoubtedly, in the flush of early enthusiasm, all sorts of untenable statements have come from child psychiatric sources. It would be purposeless at this juncture to go into the pros and cons in these pronouncements. It is of greater importance to outline some of the basic tenets that guide child psychiatry, to describe briefly how it functions and to outline some common problems.

Childhood is a period of growth, at times, during the first few years and puberty, exceptionally rapid, at others a slower process. This physical and intellectual growth will be determined partly by inherited factors, partly by the environment and partly by the history of the child since birth and even before. Thus a disease such as German measles in early pregnancy may damage the child and so may, though not necessarily, a number of obstetrical mishaps. Later on diseases affecting the brain, such as meningitis or encephalitis, may do further damage although commonly these leave no sequelae. Such a history would, of course, be of vital importance to future development. Apart from the physical health, the intellectual capacity has to be assessed. Is it average, above or below? If at the defective level, it presents its own constellation of difficulties and these are dealt with separately below. Next, the child's environment, in terms of living conditions and of the people, parents and educators who surround him, is of vital importance in his growth. Certain questions have to be asked. Is the environment satisfactory? Is the child receiving continuous and loving care adequate to meet its own particular needs? Broken homes, separated parents, institutionalization and unsatisfactory emotional relations are often the ingredients with which the psychiatrist has to work. If the home is intact and the relationship satisfactory, the expectations of the environment have to be considered. Are parents pushing their children beyond their intellectual and emotional capacities to satisfy some unreasonable aim? Is the child fighting a losing battle in trying to keep up with a more intelligent brother or sister, driven by well-meaning but mistaken parents? All this can be easily sorted out by an intelligence test which will be a reasonably good guide to the child's capabilities. A chance to meet the parents will not only reveal such unrealistic expectations but will provide an opportunity to assess their personalities and psychiatric health, both of paramount influence for the development of their child.

Broadly speaking, there are three main groups of disorders for which psychiatric help will be sought. There is the small group of children who have sustained some form of brain damage. Epilepsy, brain injuries, the sequelae from infections of the brain, may all be associated with behaviour, scholastic and physical disorder. The next, and numerically most important, will be the habits, behaviour disorders and neurotic traits. Tics, eating disturbances, enuresis, nightmares and night terrors, nail-biting, head banging, thumb-sucking, temper tantrums are the type of complaints that would come under this group. More specific neurotic manifestations, such as excessive fears of the dark, animals, water, seeking constant attention from the mother, refusal to be separated from the mother to go to school, hysterical symptoms and a few cases with frank psychotic manifestations, would also belong to this group. The remaining disorders would be labelled as conduct disturbances and would include persistent lying, wandering away from home, stealing, aimless destruction, starting fires and some offences necessitating appearance in a juvenile court.

The essential team of a child psychiatry clinic is composed of a psychiatrist, specially trained in child psychiatry, a psychologist and a psychiatric social worker, who can be of either sex but is usually a woman. The psychiatric social worker holds a degree in social science and is further trained in psychological disorders. She takes the place of the almoner in the general hospital but the training she receives equips her to deal more extensively with psychiatric problems directly, either with the parents in the case of children or with the patient and relatives in the case of adults. After the initial problem is presented, the psychiatrist in charge makes an assessment of the various factors as previously outlined and the psychologist assesses the intelligence and educational skills of the child. A programme of treatment is outlined and the child is seen separately by the doctor, while one or both parents are seen by the social worker. Rarely are the rôles reversed. Two examples have been selected to illustrate how this works in practice.

The first is that of bed-wetting or nocturnal enuresis. This is an extremely common disorder affecting both sexes but more commonly boys. A great deal of research has been undertaken on enuresis and the view is that it is the result of multiple causes.[1] Some children come from families where enuresis is prominent in their siblings and was also present in either or both parents and their relations. In other words, there is some form of hereditary basis. In many others no such explanation is present and psychological factors are more prominent. The home of the child may be unsatisfactory in that parents are living in disharmony, either or both may have deserted or died, or if living and present are cold, rejecting people unable to offer the love and security the child needs. All these categories are extremely common. There may be over-restriction and excessive demands made, against which the child rebels and can only express this revolt through its nightly incontinence. Poverty and poor social conditions are sometimes associated with enuresis[2] and may contribute to its perpetuation by unsatisfactory upbringing. Insecurity and anxiety may result from parents showing favour to a brother or sister or from poor scholastic achievement. Whatever the precipitating factors, by the time the child reaches the clinic a vicious circle has been set up. At home, everything possible will have been tried, physical remedies, bribes, rebukes, punishment, physical and psychological. In a boarding school, the attendent shame and disgrace of public discovery will have further shaken any remaining confidence of the child. Insecure, miserable and humiliated, he will have no one to turn

[1] B. Hallgren, "Enuresis, A Clinical and Genetic Study", *Acta psychiat.* (Kbh), suppl. 114 (1957).
[2] J. M. Bloomfield and J. W. B. Douglas, "Bedwetting, Prevalence among Children Aged 4–7 Years", *Lancet* (1956), I, p. 850.

to. In these circumstances, he may either give up altogether and become anxious and depressed or turn his humiliation into anger and aggression and fight with everyone. The parent, especially the mother, will by now have also been humiliated, accepting the enuresis as her fault and, although publicly disclaiming it, in all probability be inwardly blaming herself. Tensions are set up and the peace of the home severely disturbed. With this background the clinic will set to work. The psychological report will reveal the need for any readjustment at school if the scholastic load is too much. A relationship will be formed with the child. Accusations, bribes and punishments will cease, he will be encouraged to talk and, probably for the first time, he will find that someone is prepared to listen and to treat him as an individual worthy of attention. The talk will initially be halting and hesitant and may eventually lapse into complete silence. Slowly and with much patience, confidence will be gained and various subjects not particularly concerned with enuresis may be introduced initially. School, games, hobbies and special interests may be discussed and interest will be shown in everything, special praise given for attainment and achievement. Eventually the conversation will come round to bed-wetting and this will be an appropriate opportunity to release the pent-up feelings on the subject. The emotional stranglehold will be loosened with considerable relief and easing of tension. Feelings for the parents and siblings will be expressed, both warm and hostile. Distorted relations, misconceptions and misinterpretations will be judged in a new light and what was previously a pitch-black environment may now be only grey or even greyish-white. Confidence will return and so will self-esteem. The enuresis will probably improve and may even clear up. Even if this is not achieved, it will no longer be a spectre to haunt the child.

Concurrently the parent, usually the mother, is discussing the same subject with the social worker. She will be glad to have a sympathetic listener because it is not easy to discuss the shameful deeds of your child with your next-door neighbour. Her feelings, anger, anxiety and uncertainty will be expressed. Initial fears and expectations of being reprimanded will dissolve when she receives no such reproof. Gaining confidence, she may retrace, indeed she will be encouraged to do so, her own childhood and her own relationship with her parents. Patterns do repeat themselves and she may recognize in her actions the unsuccessful habits of her own parents. Alternatively, she may see that the upbringing of her own child has led to excesses in order to repair or avoid her own childhood experiences. She may recognize that in her zeal to bring up her children correctly, love and affection have been replaced by unnecessary restraints or sometimes over-indulgence. She will be helped to reassess her current marital, social or financial difficulties and her personal anxieties and fears with their toll on her energy, time and attention for her children. All or any of these issues will be discussed and modification effected whenever possible. The father's attitude, his rôle and participation in the care of his children, is of equal importance and wherever possible he will be included in any explorations that are likely to ease the tension and in any plans for the future.

With a successful outcome, once again a relaxation, return to self-esteem and confidence can be expected and a more satisfactory parent–child relationship resumed. In a proportion of cases, cessation of the enuresis may thus follow, in others a distinct improvement; in all, one can expect an amelioration in personal relationships and a return to the proper exchange of love and security between child and parent.

The second example is less common but produces a more profound disturbance in the home situation. It concerns the problem of school refusal or school phobia, a disturbance which is increasingly seen in child psychiatry. It is also the type of issue that draws the cynical remarks of all those who have played truant some time in their school career, paid the price and were none the worse for it. School refusal and truancy are entirely different issues.[3] Truants spend their time away from school but also from home, their whereabouts unknown, until discovered by their parents or teachers. They enjoy their escapade, pay the penalties and commonly return to school. The episodes may be repeated but are rarely protracted. Truants come from homes with backgrounds of discord, broken and unsatisfactory homes, their work record at school is unsatisfactory for very often they are bored and dissatisfied with scholastic chores. The school-refuser trembles at the idea of leaving his doorstep. Starting school, when he changes from a primary to a secondary school at eleven or the beginning of a new term are the precipitating occasions and the refusal will continue day after day, extend to weeks and even months. Rebukes, bribes, scoldings and punishments, juvenile court appearances will make no difference. This will be initially interpreted as stubbornness but will frequently emerge as a morbid anxiety at being separated from mother. At school, the work is above average and often enjoyed but when the refusal commences an overwhelming anxiety gets a grip on the child and he may have to follow his mother from room to room, never letting her out of sight, as the only way to reassure himself. Examination of the parental attitudes will reveal a variety of patterns; an over-indulgent, over-anxious mother with a placid retiring father; a domineering, over-controlling mother with a similar type of father or a strong-willed domineering father with a retiring over-indulging mother. Frequently the mother will exhibit fears of her own about being left alone or of being in a crowd. Whatever the combination of circumstances, nothing else than prolonged therapy as an in-patient or out-patient along the lines described for enuresis is possible. Treatment of this kind has a good chance of success.

[3] L. A. Hersov, "Persistent Non-Attendance at School", *Journal of Child Psychology and Psychiatry* (1960), I, p. 2.

CONDUCT DISORDERS

Behaviour under this category would, *par excellence*, fit the hitherto prevailing notion that it deserved reprimand and the only successful solution for it was discipline and more discipline. To substitute the psychiatric couch for the rod is a social revolution which affronts tradition and common sense, particularly since it has yet to be shown that this innovation has any overwhelming advantage to offer. The psychiatric answer to these views would be as follows. There is no doubt that misbehaviour has taken place in the past, and will do so again in the future, in the absence of emotional disorder. This does not warrant the certainty that the two are never linked together and in practice the combination is found sufficiently often to recommend a psychiatric assessment when there are sufficient grounds. The examination and management would pursue very much the same lines as already outlined and right at the very start the intelligence of the child would be assessed, which, on more than one occasion, will be the vital clue in explaining its conduct. There are no *a priori* reasons to refute the possibility that emotional stresses and strains may in one case produce well-known neurotic disturbances and in another express themselves in antisocial behaviour and sometimes in both. The error would be to conclude that all such conduct is exclusively emotionally motivated, but this is a presumption far in excess of any current psychiatric knowledge or serious claim.

ADOLESCENCE

This is a period of rapid growth, physically, socially and psychologically. The body is assuming its definitive characteristics and the powerful sexual urges are coming to the fore. The range and quality of social contacts expand. Friendships are abandoned and new ones formed, unstable but in keeping with the spirit of adventure and discovery. The home and the next-door neighbour will prove insufficient boundaries, and the neighbourhood and further afield will be rapidly explored for its potential talent. Psychologically, the feature that stands out is the multiple expression of independence. Parents, teachers, all forms of authority are disagreeable and will be flouted to a greater or lesser degree. There are few households with teenagers who will not be aware of this transformation. A mixture of tolerance, humour and firmness will negotiate the vast majority of these instances. But in a small number a *modus vivendi* will not be found and when the child has run away from home, become involved in a flagrant promiscuous act or broken the law, psychiatric help will be invoked. A proportion of these cases will be showing frank evidence of psychiatric disturbances either of the schizophrenic or affective disorder.

In the absence of clear-cut psychotic or neurotic disturbances, there is left a residue of families which are least prepared to meet the transformation of adolescence. If the relationship between parents and children is seen from the very beginning as a journey of gradual separation with the parental rôle as a unique opportunity to foster and develop the God-given gifts of each individual child for its ultimate full and responsible independence, the threshold of this achievement will hold few complete surprises. Adolescence will be the final stages of this progress and will not be without some distress to both parties. The child will be pulled in two directions, forwards towards adulthood, driven by the excessive energy which he is experiencing, but which is also frightening because of the lack of experience in handling it, backwards towards the security and warmth of parents and home. This divided loyalty, which has to be overcome in some form of separation, has its own price of suffering before a successful conclusion. What appears outwardly as stubbornness, defiance, callousness and indifference is not infrequently a precarious externalization of inward doubt, misery and strife. The parents, and particularly the mother, are loth to abandon what may have become a pivot of their existence. If all else fails, resort is made to further repressive measures until the fatal moment is reached when submission is totally revoked. The task of the psychiatrist is to conciliate. To the parents, he can offer his help by outlining the processes involved and by reassuring and removing their fears and doubts. To the adolescent, he can extend the sort of support which acknowledges the pending independence but avoids the rejection of values and all authority.

Two issues are sources of particular apprehension to the Christian family. The first is the emergence of sexual activity. The form this will take, both in its physical expression and psychological appreciation, will depend very much on the handling of this question throughout childhood. Christian teaching has always asserted that sexual instruction is an individual matter and incorporates much more than biological knowledge. No growth of understanding, which has not love as its centre, can ever claim to fulfil adequately the spiritual, psychological and physical requirements of this subject. What has not always been clear is how this instruction is to be effected and what the content should be. While each family and each child are individuals who require modifications to meet their particular needs, it is generally agreed that it is the serenity, peace and love of the home which supply the framework and example, within which increasing information is imparted with advancing age. It has to be admitted that this has not always been successfully accomplished in the past and a veil of secrecy and ignorance has surrounded sex. It would indeed be surprising if the transition from such a silent vacuum to the explosion of adolescence could take place without some turbulence. The adolescent overvalues the body while all those surrounding him undervalue it. If tuition has been adequate and the family background a living expression of love and temperance, there will be no need to undervalue the temple of the Holy Spirit nor will the adolescent misinterpret the urgent calls of the body as the only message that matters.

The second subject is lapsing from the practice of religious duties, with the ultimate loss of faith. It is widely recognized that, while religious practices may be abandoned at any time, adolescence is a particularly vulnerable period. The reasons offered for such an event are many and include intellectual doubts, poor example set at home, inadequate religious training at school, long-standing indifferences with superficial adherence due to scholastic pressure now no longer available and many others. All these factors may be operating in some instances but is it a chance coincidence that adolescence and the second half of the second decade are peak periods for abandoning the practice of religion? Is it not possible to consider these lapses as psychological phenomena linked with a period of rebellion and rejection? The growth of religion as a psychological phenomenon with its vulnerable periods is one of the most urgent tasks for investigation facing the Christian psychologist. The fruits of such research will yield knowledge of mutual benefit both to psychology and religion, particularly in relation to chronological, critical periods in childhood, adolescence and middle age.

MENTAL DEFICIENCY

Mental deficiency was one of the earliest subjects to receive systematic study at the hands of psychologists and psychiatrists. The work was facilitated by the invention and widespread use of intelligence tests, providing an objective and reliable method of classification. The French psychologist, Binet, devised the first tests at the beginning of this century and, with continuous refinement, they have become an invaluable tool for the assessment of mental retardation. When the intelligence of an unselected population is tested in this way, it is found to have a normal curve of distribution; that is to say, the majority of people are of an intelligence quotient (I.Q.) on or near 100, which is the average, with progressively smaller percentages covering the deviations, both above and below the mean. An arbitrary figure of 70 and below has been chosen to designate the level of mental deficiency and it is estimated that approximately one per cent of the children in Great Britain belong to this category.[4] Until recently one standard way of tackling this problem was to build large institutions and to house therein the maximum number of patients. Research is beginning to show that, although this method may have economic advantages, it is the least satisfactory for the backward child, who needs more rather than less individual attention. When the latter approach has been put into effective operation, it has met with considerable success.[5] The upper-grade mental defective (50–70 I.Q.) benefits sufficiently to be able to cope with simple jobs and to maintain a satisfactory and economically independent status in the community. Scholastic tuition needs to be radically transformed from the traditional approaches to meet the special needs of these children. Not only the rate and amount of comprehension but the subjects have to be different. The learning of cleanliness, dressing, the ability to travel, to carry out simple monetary transactions and a rudimentary acquaintance with the "three R's" are key subjects which, if attained to a sufficient degree, allow a considerable measure of independence. They are all certainly attainable with practice. These achievements in social adaptation should provide the stimulus for Christian research workers to study suitable means by which these children can be taught the concepts of God, moral values and the elementary rudiments of the Christian heritage. The achievement of a level of sufficiency which will transform these children from passive to more active agents in their spiritual destiny is a worthy and challenging task.

Intimately associated with mental deficiency are the problems of marriage and procreation concerning these retarded

[4] E. O. Lewis, "Report of the Mental Deficiency Committee" (1929); W. Mayer-Gross, "Mental Health Survey in a Rural Area—A preliminary report", *Eugenic Review* (1948), p. 40.

[5] J. Tizard, *B.M.J.* (1960), I, p. 1041.

citizens when they reach adulthood. Surveys in the last thirty years have shown fairly consistently that the size of the family and intelligence are intimately connected. High parental intelligence goes hand in hand with small families and vice versa. This has led to gloomy forecasts about a drop in the average intelligence as the less intelligent outnumber the rest with their size of family.[6] When these fears were coupled with the knowledge that the ranks of criminals, juvenile delinquents, prostitutes and all sorts of social destitutes are swollen considerably by mental defectives, it can be appreciated that at the social level an eugenic campaign in favour of sterilization gathered momentum in several countries. Recent studies have not confirmed the original fears about the drop of intelligence.[7] This is due to many factors among which is a well-recognized one for the I.Q. to veer towards the mean. That is to say, children of very bright parents will be less so and children of the less gifted more so. An impressive study has been recently concluded on this point. Seventy-three mothers, all of them previously patients of a mentally defective institution, with an average I.Q. of 73·5, were followed over a period of twenty years. Altogether they had 150 children, forty-one of whom died. The mean I.Q. of those who survived was 91·2.[8] The other feature that has been shown by recent work is the lower marriage rate of the mentally retarded, one result showing only half the rate of a comparable normal population.[9] Another point of relevance in connection with sterilization and mental defect is an increasing knowledge of the sources of mental defectives. One source has already been indicated. This is a small percentage who might be expected to have a low I.Q. on the basis of the normal distribution of intelligence in society. The other is from conditions deter-

[6] C. Burt, *Intelligence and Fertility*, London (1946).

[7] Scottish Council for Research in Education, *The Trend of Scottish Intelligence*, London (1949); *Social Implications of the 1947 Scottish Mental Survey*, London (1953).

[8] M. W. G. Brandon, *Journal of Mental Science* (1957), CIII, p. 710.

[9] F. Visser, *Mensch en Maatsch.* (1936), XII, p. 416.

mined by specific genes. Very few of these are handed down from generation to generation. The majority appear spontaneously and their prevention does not lie with eugenic sterilization.

All these reasons have damped the ardour of the sterilization enthusiasts and current medical opinion is in agreement with the authoritative statement of Professor Penrose, a world authority on this subject, whose view is that the genetic constitution of future generations is not likely to be jeopardized by allowing fertile high-grade defectives to have offspring.[10] This is a conclusion which is in complete agreement with the Christian belief that sterilization in the absence of adequate medical reasons offends against the law of nature. This, however, does not mean that mental defectives should be encouraged to have large families. Such mothers are gravely handicapped in the upbringing of their children and the high mortality quoted above is one measure of the parental inefficiency found in these families. Frequently, closely spaced pregnancies easily exhaust their limited capacities. They would undoubtedly come under the category for family limitation outlined by Pius XII in his address on the subject. Mere advice on how this should be effected will often prove futile unless it is backed by close support and supervision from all social agencies, statutory and voluntary.

[10] L. S. Penrose, "Propagation of the Unfit", *Lancet* (1950), II, p. 425.

CHAPTER IX

RESPONSIBILITY

References have been made in previous chapters to various issues which have a particular relationship to moral responsibility. In this chapter an attempt will be made to clarify the general principles which govern Christian thought in this matter. In a period of history when man is about to conquer outer space and has mastered energy to an unprecedented degree, it is not surprising to find so much concentration on his potential here and now. Although the Christian shares this preoccupation, the essentials of his beliefs demand a continuous awareness of his eternal destiny. What appears to even the sympathetic observer as a morbid and at times irrelevant preoccupation with details is, in practice, the persistent search for the means of absorbing psychiatric truths in a way that will not violate the natural law and God's revealed truth. To those who do not share these basic tenets, we must extend a friendly and sincere respect while they in turn must be patient and accord us the right to seek truth in the light of our faith.

The essentials of human responsibility in Christian ethics presuppose in man a rational being endowed with a will and capable of free choice in the presence of alternative modes of conduct based ultimately on absolute norms present in the mind of God. Diametrically opposed to this view is determinism. This view has been stated succinctly recently by Dr Maddison[1] who says: "Determinism implies that human

[1] David C. Maddison, *Lancet* (1959), II, p. 103.

behaviour is inexorably governed by the dynamic interplay upon the individual of numerous forces derived from his genetic background, biological constitution, emotional development and unresolved needs and goals, many of which may not be accessible to ordinary consciousness." He goes on to add that in this framework of psychoanalytical theory "morality", the existence of "good and bad" must be regarded as the products of the human mind and therefore presumably subject only to biological and psychological investigation.

There is here a fundamental cleavage of two systems, one demanding as a necessity a Supreme Creator from whom is derived an order of values which man, by his very nature, is fundamentally free to operate either by rejection or acceptance. The other, totally excluding this order, places man at the head of the hierarchy and draws its values from the changing development of intellect and environment. This is not the place to argue the evidence for and against these theses and in any case when all the arguments have been examined the final choice for either side depends in practice on an act of faith.

It is important, however, for Christian thought and practice to examine the growing knowledge which psychology has unfolded on the nature of man and to incorporate the indisputable features in its own framework.

Responsibility, we have seen, implies adequate and rational knowledge and the exercise of a free will. The first stage that has to be defined is the age of attaining reason. Moral theologians have as one of their primary tasks to be precise and, with this obligation in mind, various ages have been arbitrarily assigned as the arrival point for the age of reason and therefore for responsibility. From what we know about child development, as for any process of growth, it is abundantly clear that although it is useful to have an average figure, it is a fundamental error to assign the qualities of the average to the particular person. There cannot be any rigidity, that is, a child has reached this or that age and therefore must be responsible for this or that matter. Each child follows an unique biological and spiritual development and its awareness may be accelerated or retarded depending on a host of constitutional and environmental factors. It is imperative that no child, and for that matter no person, should ever be subjected to moral edicts beyond his comprehension, and only considerable knowledge of the individual will reveal his particular stage of attainment. The wide range of individual variation must never be forgotten and never be subjected to arbitrary divisions appropriate to theoretical concepts.

There are two clear instances where rational knowledge is lacking with proportionate diminution of responsibility. The first is the limitations secondary to mental defect, and the other is clear-cut psychotic episodes, examples of which will be given below. In the past, moral theologians have tended to adopt the attitude that in the presence of an evil, if the person possessed full cognitive knowledge of the nature of the evil and exercised his free will by giving full consent to it, then a sinful action was committed, its gravity and subjective responsibility depending on the nature of the action. Modern theological opinion has now come to accept that, even in the presence of full cognitive knowledge, there is an additional factor required, namely an adequate appraisal or evaluation of an action in terms of its intrinsic moral worth. Evaluation means an appreciative assessment by a person of the goodness, value and relationship of an act to God's plan for man. With an increased blurring of evaluation, there is a diminishing responsibility. It is of course impossible to assess subjective responsibility in absolute terms in this situation, and in these circumstances judgements should be cautious. In the field of psychiatric disorder, this matter of evaluation is of greatest importance for here we are dealing with a range of propensities, richly charged with emotional and psychological values, deeply imbedded in the personality. There may be present an order of valuation that may clash seriously with the objective moral law and may require a considerable reorientation both spiritual and psychological before the comprehension of an act corresponds sufficiently with the objectivity of the moral assessment. To give but one example here, the homosexual has grown up in a psychological and social atmosphere in which he comes to accept an order of sexual meaning diametrically opposed to that of theology and Western society. Although his overt sexual behaviour is objectively and gravely wrong, it does not necessarily imply that with each violation he is subjectively responsible to the same degree. His assessment of a particular situation may be different and, although he may know that what he is doing is contrary to the law of God, in fact it may be extremely difficult for him to appreciate the value of alternative behaviour. Although this does not automatically excuse his behaviour, which remains objectively at variance with the moral law, it would be incorrect to pass adverse automatic judgement on his subjective responsibility without a good deal of knowledge of his understanding and appraisal of his actions.

In addition to the individual's biological, psychological and spiritual development which will be the ultimate contribution to evaluation, there are certain epochs in life which add particular obstacles to the realization of unimpeachable assessment and rational judgement. The period of childhood has already been mentioned and usually allowances are made at this stage. Adolescence is the next phase and the one which receives the least sympathetic understanding. Under the shape of adulthood masquerade a confusion and uncertainty which baffle both the adolescent and the adult whose expectations are guided by the misjudged external appearances. Particularly, but not exclusively, in the sexual field the storm of growth, emotional and physical, makes evaluation of behaviour an extremely confusing matter and responsibility must, here more than at any other time, be judged with the discretion which springs from the intimate knowledge of the individual rather than from absolute judicial edicts. Old age is often the culmination of the rich fruits of experience and wisdom. On the other hand individuals vary enormously in the timing of some intellectual falling off, some blunting in judgement. When behaviour surprises and shocks at this age, it is invariably wise to think of an early dementing process which has effected enough deterioration to contract full responsibility to something less.

Beyond the fringe of knowledge and evaluation, another reason for diminished responsibility is to be found in those situations where the freedom of action is diminished. Theologians have always recognized that passions may overwhelm the person suddenly and completely to the point where freedom of choice does not exist and responsibility is not present. Outbursts of anger, fear, excitement, aggression may overtake the normal person on rare occasions in the presence of sufficiently grave incitement. It can easily be appreciated that in the presence of a psychiatric disturbance, which includes pathological features that lend themselves to such outbursts, their frequency will be greater and the responsibility reduced proportionately. It should be emphasized that these psychiatric disturbances do not *ipso facto* absolve the person from responsibility, the need to avoid provoking occasions and to seek suitable psychiatric help if this is available.

Finally, it is also recognized that the establishment of a habit facilitates the subsequent repetition of an action. Understandably, acceptable habits present no problems, but occasions of immoral conduct do. Theologians have always allowed some diminution of responsibility with established habits, which produce for a time a constitutional vulnerability of such an order that moral defeat can be the only outcome for short or long periods. Psychological work has amply demonstrated the facilitating process of repetition and has supported the traditional view of the presence of an inhibition for the opposite desired effect. But psychiatry has gone further and seeks to find the motives for habits and the needs which are being fulfilled by their presence. A pastor may be satisfied with the spiritual efforts of a person who is trying to break a particularly bad habit but dissatisfied with his progress in mastering it. When ordinary efforts appear unsuccessful, psychiatric help may be advantageous. It will be able to explore the emotional and psychological reasons behind the habit, bring to the surface conscious and unconscious conflicts and in this way may resolve the underlying tensions which feed it.

PSYCHOSES

Psychotic illnesses, as indicated in Chapter III, produce profound disturbances, among other things in mood, feelings, perception and thought. Since responsible behaviour presupposes intact intellectual, physical and emotional processes, grave violations of the moral law can take place in the presence of these pathological conditions without incurring subjective responsibility. Suicide in depressive illness is perhaps one of the commonest. Homicide, however, can occur both in schizophrenia at the instigation of auditory hallucinations which demand the killing of some person, and in depressive illness where the patient includes his spouse, children or relatives in the wave of hopelessness which may overtake him. Paranoid schizophrenics can commit heinous crimes following the dictates of their paranoid delusions. Epileptic attacks can reduce a man's normal control severely and be followed by irresponsible and bizarre behaviour. It is true that with modern therapy these episodes should diminish for all psychotic illnesses but in none of these instances can imputability be ascribed to the sufferer.

NEUROTIC AND PERSONALITY DISORDERS

In these conditions there is a lack of the florid pathological features that are present in psychotic illness. In personality disorders there is present a complicated interplay of genetic, constitutional and psychological factors which combine to produce a wide range of deviation. It is difficult to assess precisely in given cases how much these factors influence habitual behaviour which contravenes the moral law and impedes spiritual progress. In some cases, an assessment is not difficult. Persistent psychopathic behaviour shows a lack of evaluation which may extend from a total absence to various degrees of diminution of the moral worth of an action. Again a paranoid person who, by definition, is prone to misjudge people with the consequent expectation of hostile and adverse response from them, is handling innumerable life situations with a psychological deficit which is bound to diminish to a certain extent his responsibility for his behaviour. Morbid jealousy is yet another example which is an affliction not obviously a psychiatric illness and yet crippling in its impact on human relations. Despite considerable efforts, it may prove unresponsive to treatment and may be responsible for marriage breakdowns and much unhappiness to many people. In all these character or personality disturbances the morbid temperament cannot be the excuse or the signal for wrong behaviour. But where such behaviour occurs adequate allowances have to be made for it.

Moving from these personality disturbances into the clearly defined neurotic illnesses described in Chapter IV, there is present a clearer delineation for a morbid process and it becomes easier to establish criteria for responsibility. The commonest and most obvious example is the obsessional-compulsive illness. Here the essential pathology is a process of compulsion either for a thought or an action against which in the severe stage of the illness the patient cannot exercise his free will, and has no control over his behaviour. In these circumstances, however much he may internally resist the dictates of the compulsion, he is unable to overcome it. It is quite clear that, if any part or all of the obsessive-compulsive processes included material that violated the dictates of the moral law, there would not be any subjective responsibility. Such assessments however have to be made in co-operation with the psychiatrist who is attending the patient and who is the only person likely to be in full possession of all the relevant facts.

Phobias may be so severe at times that a person is unable to join a crowd and therefore unable to attend to the liturgical requirements of his faith. Once again we are dealing with a pathological process and the same applies if the neuroses express themselves in the form of an acute panic or anxiety attack in certain situations.

The problem of hysteria versus malingering has already been alluded to. In both these situations the patient stands to gain some advantage by the clinical state, and the classical criterion of differentiation is the presence or absence of conscious and deliberate intention to feign the symptoms. Not infrequently this is an issue in cases which are diagnosed as suffering from complete loss of memory of certain details in their past life. It is common to find in retrospect that they are usually running away from an impossible situation at home or at work or from the consequences of some crime. Sometimes it is impossible to assess whether the patient is feigning amnesia and under such conditions it is tempting to decide against the person, if he is known to have committed some crime, and to give him the benefit of the doubt in the absence of anti-social behaviour. Since it is possible but unproven that the mechanisms which produce amnesia are the same, independent of the precipitating circumstances, and there is an admixture of conscious and unconscious motivation, one should be extremely wary making absolute pronouncements in these cases.

SEXUAL PROBLEMS

It is under this category more than any other that Christian thought has become disturbed at the apparent loosening of the moral principles under the impact of psychiatric theory. The considerable advances in psychoanalytic thought have been linked with Freud's theory of sexuality and there has developed a confusion between legitimate psychological theory and a vague sexual hygiene which draws its strength more from the inspiration of misinformed would-be reformers than from established psychiatric principles.

As was indicated before, there is considerable confusion between the concepts of repression and suppression. Whereas Freud and subsequent psychiatric practice have given careful attention to those psychological matters, including sexual, in the life of the individual which, although not conscious, exert an adverse influence, no one has shown that outside this pathological field the normal processes of self-discipline in the sexual field, attained by suppression, have a similar pathological influence. On the available evidence, psychiatry offers no support or any acceptable foundation for the disruption of accepted Christian sexual ethics.

There are, however, sexual matters which have been illuminated by psychiatric advance. Homosexuality and all other perversions are now clearly to be seen within the orbit of abnormal behaviour which may have as its basis pathological psychological processes. As far as responsibility is concerned, each individual person must be assessed on the merits of the particular instance. The nature of the deviation, the psychological disturbances behind it, the age of the person (and here we must remember the impact of adolescence and old age), the presence and strength of established habits, the recognition and evaluation of the action concerned and the efforts of the individual to overcome the difficulty will all have a bearing on the responsibility for individual acts. It can be seen that only an intimate knowledge of the person will help to assess all these issues and close cooperation between pastor and psychiatrist is of great importance. Masturbation is a particular subject that causes a great deal of difficulty. If the factors of age, knowledge and evaluation are taken into consideration, often enough in practice the assessment will be less grave than would appear at first sight. Persistent masturbation after puberty and adolescence is a different issue which may indicate a seriously disturbed personality needing expert help.

CONCLUSION

The laws of morality are framed with the uniform growth of human potentialities and the average normal man and woman in mind. They give clear-cut definitions, as of necessity they must do, to avoid confusion and to reflect the absolute truths from which their source is derived. It is a matter of everyday experience that their application is flexible and must meet the limitations of human potentialities which are found in practice. While the objectivity of the law remains intact, its flexibility must increase, particularly in psychiatric problems as one shifts from the normal by increasing degrees to the abnormal. If the application of the law to these patients appears at times to have little relation to its absolute edicts, it must be remembered that this is only done after careful consideration of what the sick in mind can be reasonably expected to practise, given their particular deficiencies.

CHAPTER X

THE RÔLE OF THE PRIEST

Psychiatry and religion have man as a common object for study and effective action. What the precise boundaries of their respective rôles are is a matter of argument and controversy and in practice there are many areas where precise definitions are not possible. In this confused and blurred arena, the suggestion has been expressed that one way to solve the difficulty is for the priest to assume the dual rôle of therapist and pastor. This is a view with which the author is totally out of sympathy. Before we can discuss the relevant issues, it is as well to have a clear concept of what the two vocations, of the priesthood and of psychiatry, entail.

The functions of a priest are clearly laid down by the bishop before ordination. They are to offer sacrifice, bless, preside, preach and baptize. As Fr Carré says, the essentials with which the priest is concerned are worship and teaching.[1] As shepherd of his flock, minister of divine worship, and servant of love (*Codex Juris Canonici*, can. 948) he has other duties to perform but the fringe must not be confused with the central part of his work. Psychiatry imposes different requirements. Usually a medical qualification is required, and when analytical psychotherapy is undertaken by the layman, it should be done in conjunction with a trained medical psychiatrist who has made an initial diagnostic assessment. Those who favour the dual rôle of the priest are primarily concerned with the psychotherapeutic part of psychiatry. This is to forget that psychiatry is firmly embedded in the domain

[1] A. M. Carré, *The Everlasting Priest*, London (1960), pp. 30–45.

of medicine and is concerned essentially with disturbances of the physis, both physical and psychological. Any attempt to isolate a part of this work from the main field is depriving the patient of the increasing benefits of pharmacological and other agents which, when used with care, can be advantageous in the management of a neurosis. In addition, the central core of psychotherapy is a meaningful relationship which can comprise orthodox Freudian transference but also include a host of other dependent, infantile and essentially disturbed needs which require solution. To be able to achieve a therapeutic effect in such a rôle, the priest must of necessity effectively abandon the rôle of his vocation and assume a different task. Leaving aside the innumerable psychological difficulties in this substitution of rôles, in this other capacity he would be denying the fundamentals of his priestly functions.

On the other hand, the Church is increasingly aware of continuous change in society and of the need for the priest to familiarize himself with these developments. One of the undoubted transformations is the growing knowledge of the content and causes of psychiatric illnesses and it is no longer possible for the priest to remain aloof from this subject if he is to maintain the essential intimate contact with his flock. Nearly half the total National Health Service hospital beds in Great Britain are occupied by patients with psychiatric illnesses and those who are not sick enough to be in hospital, but sufficiently disturbed to be in real distress, are many. From this vast army of sufferers, the priest who, with his outstretched hands, must try to encompass the love of the Eternal Priest, cannot stand aloof. The complete answer of how best he can serve without losing his identity has yet to be worked out, and in any case will differ from locality to locality. The exact definition of the priest's rôle in this as in all matters is primarily in the hands of the bishop of the diocese. All that a layman can do is to assist in the task by presenting clearly the needs of this work and the conditions under which it can be done.

To begin with, a certain amount of basic knowledge is required. Although this can be derived from books, it seems to the author infinitely more valuable if, at the appropriate stage of the priest's training, a well-informed and competent psychiatrist can bring together the basic information and relate it to the broad and specific Christian issues with which psychiatry is concerned. This leads on to the converse side of the coin, namely the need for practising Christian psychiatrists to be not only thoroughly competent in their own special subjects but sufficiently informed and aware of the basic moral and theological issues. This is absolutely essential not only for the benefit of the patient but as a means of closing the appalling gap in semantic communication between the two disciplines.

In the parish, a priest prepared with this information will have the great advantage of recognizing from the very onset when he is dealing with a psychiatrically disturbed patient. He can then work in conjunction with the psychiatrist in an exchange of meaningful and complementing information and help. If the priest knows that this particular member of his flock is suffering from this or that psychiatric disturbance, he will be sufficiently forearmed not to waste his energy, for example, in trying to alter delusions nor to ignore the essential pathology of obsessional rumination and neurotic guilt. On the contrary, working in conjunction with the psychiatrist, he can continually adjust the spiritual goals of the patient, keeping them sufficiently high not to remove the efficacy of religion from the grasp of the patient, at the same time avoiding standards and expectations which are beyond his reach and which may extinguish the flickering light of faith in the abyss of despair. Imbued with charity, which comes from the fullness of understanding, the priest can now with firmness, now with flexibility, but always with patience and compassion, remind the patient of his duties. While taking full cognizance of his difficulties, he can help him to participate as fully as possible in the life of the Church.

Participation in the life of the Church brings up the crucial question of what effect the life of grace can be expected to have on psychiatric illness. There are still those who will insist that, for a great deal of psychiatric disturbance, all that is required is the conscientious effort of the will, harvesting the benefit of prayer, good works and the frequent reception of the sacraments.

No one expects grace by itself to restore a broken limb or heal a tuberculous lesion, yet it is expected that this is the only requirement to cure an obsessional neurosis, attacks of anxiety or a depressive illness. This is a grave misconception and springs from the inability to accept these disorders as truly genuine ailments. While it is perfectly true that grace perfects nature, its primary aim is not to restore the disintegrated physiological and psychological fragments of man responsible for disease. Fr Victor White sums up this matter thus:

> Its function (grace) is still to perfect and bring health and wholeness to human nature, and this precisely by restoring its centre of cohesion in God. Baptism brings forgiveness and the rebirth of the life of grace which original sin had lost. But it does not automatically restore the prototypal integrity. It is empirically evident enough that, as the Council of Trent pointed out, baptism does not straightaway cure the disorder of desire, the disintegration of tendencies which results from the loss of the original innocence and equilibrium. Still less does it eliminate the particular causes of particular disorders, nor is it directly concerned with them. They remain the specific province of medicine whether somatic or psychological.[2]

But while the psychiatrist is busy applying his knowledge and skill, it is abundantly clear that the restoration of the centre of cohesion in God must go on. Psychiatric disturbances by their persistence and widespread involvement of the personality have a greater tendency than physical ailments to

[2] Victor White, *Soul and Psyche*, London (1960), pp. 185-6.

remove the patient's attention from God to himself. Destructive introspection is a common accompaniment of psychiatric illness, the patient gradually losing himself in a sea of self-pity. Therapy can mitigate this as far as possible but the priest can, in conjunction with the physician, inspire and encourage the spiritual goals appropriate to the person. We are all bidden to seek perfection as far as possible and this goal remains just as appropriate for the sick as for the healthy. Sometimes no more can be done for the patient than to help him to accept his disability and it may well be that this is the particular cross God wants him to bear. With the help of his pastor, he can be helped to integrate his suffering in his life and to see it as the instrument of his perfection. To achieve this will require patience, perseverance and spiritual guidance of a high order, challenging tasks, fitted to the priestly vocation.

Finally, a word should be said about the religious outlook of the psychiatrist. One of the essential links in psychiatric therapy is the relationship between doctor and patient. If in practice it is not often possible that the two should share common backgrounds and values, it is incumbent upon the practitioner, and in practice carried out as far as possible, to make an effort to appreciate the differences which the patient expresses. When Christian principles are at issue, ideally doctor and patient should not disagree on fundamentals, for the doctor will not then command the patient's confidence which is of such great importance. As has already been stated, most psychiatrists carrying out their work conscientiously try as far as possible to communicate meaningfully with the patient even on issues on which they hold different views. At times, of course, the patient's requirements may be of a kind demanding a depth and range of Christian issues outside the experience of the particular doctor. In these cases a transfer to a doctor who is aware of the particular problem will be advantageous.

CHAPTER XI

CHRISTIANITY AND
PSYCHIATRY

Psychiatry is comparatively one of the newest branches of modern medicine. The great advances which began to unify psychological diseases into acceptable descriptive units, thus putting an end to the hitherto diagnostic chaos, date only from the last quarter of the last century. Since then, progress has been continuous, now slow, now rapid, but never returning to the previous disorganization. During the same time, Freud stamped the genius of his work on the subject. The novelty of his theories and the result of his researches have undoubtedly dominated much of the thought on the subject and have gained enormous popularity in society at large. With this latter development in mind, it is not surprising that there has grown mistrust, suspicion and antagonism between psychiatric and Christian thought, which has often exhausted the energies of both on themes outside strictly clinical issues. The philosophy of psychoanalysis contradicts many of the fundamental beliefs of Christianity and this in turn has provoked angry and at times irrelevant rebukes. In this exchange the subject matter of psychiatry—psychological disorders—has often been bypassed to the detriment of all concerned.

Freud compared himself with Copernicus and Darwin, bringing about through his discoveries of the unconscious a revolution whereby man was dethroned from the kingdom of absolute conscious control of his environment. He showed, and no one has contradicted his findings, the enormous importance of man's unconscious in his everyday activities of thought and action. Carried to its extreme conclusion, Freud and his followers have seen in this discovery the end of free will, which is one of the cornerstones of the Christian concept of man. It must be remembered that the evidence gathered in favour of such absolute determinism originates from material derived from sick people. The tendency to generalize from the particular to the general is always dangerous, and becomes acutely so when the transfer is from the sick to the healthy. These generalizations are inadmissible and are not supported by any scientifically accepted evidence. The Freudian view of absolute determinism is as strong and as plausible as its adherents are in their desire to find an alternative to theism. To deny its existence is no biased disavowal; no sound and indisputable scientific evidence exists which is contradicted.

Even when determinism in this way is not a problem, the discovery of the unconscious has presented, nonetheless, a veiled threat which Christians find difficult to absorb into their philosophy. But why this distrust of a discovery which advances so profoundly man's knowledge of himself? Is man any poorer for knowing more about the source and depth of his emotional and intellectual life? Is his service to God and his neighbour in any way diminished by the extended boundaries of his psychological life? Surely not. Science has given us the key to one more secret lock in our nature. In the presence of disease, psychoanalysis has given us yet one more weapon to fight with and, as a research tool, it provides the means of further valuable advances. Indeed, Jung's researches by this technique have thrown considerable light on the universality of man's religious sense and the use that is made of symbols, rites and beliefs. Pius XII had this to say on the subjcet: "We should certainly not find fault with depth psychology, if it deals with the psychic aspect of religious phenomena and endeavours to analyse and reduce it to a scientific system, even if this research and its terminology was not in use in times past."[1]

Much of the antagonism to psychoanalysis springs from Freud's concept of the origins of religion and civilization. He postulates a primordial murder, the killing of the primal father. The scene is set with the father of the tribe being the sole and jealous possessor of his wives, his sons not allowed to indulge their desires on them. Filled with anger and passion, the sons combine and kill the father. But then fear and remorse set in, fear that they in turn will be killed when they fulfil their sexual desire on the dead father's wives, and remorse for the killing. Civilization now rises from the prevention of sexual satisfaction with the mother, the transformation of this desire into acceptable channels and aggression away from others. God becomes the projected desire to reinstate the father, becoming in due course the God of Judaism and Christianity. In all this we see, of course, the theoretical framework behind the oedipal complex and Freud's two primary instinctual drives, sexuality and aggression. As for the myth itself, let Freud himself evaluate its validity: "I am not an ethnologist, but a psychoanalyst. . . . It is my good right to select from ethnological data what would serve me for my analytical work."[2]

The instinctual theories of sexuality and aggression operating in the framework of the pleasure principle are clearly inadequate to describe the complexity of man and have been justly criticized by other analysts. No one outside the very orthodox Freudian school pretends that they are more than part of the truth. But part of the truth they certainly are, as histories of countless patients will reveal. In this respect they present both a challenge and an opportunity for Christianity. The challenge lies in the necessary reorientation which Christianity will have to make to the discoveries of the sexual rôle in the development of the child. Sexuality does

[1] Pius XII, Catholic Documents, Psychotherapy and Clinical Psychology, XII (1953).

[2] S. Freud, *Moses and Monotheism*, Hogarth Press (1939), p. 207.

not begin in adolescence. By that time, patterns of emotional importance have been established between the child and his parents. These are carried over and will influence adult behaviour. The same applies to the instincts of aggression, anger and hostility. That these emotions are present in man has always been known. But their presence in infancy, their development, their relationship to sexuality, their partial flight into the unconscious and the intricate nuances of their growth are the subject of detailed psychological researches. We cannot be satisfied to accept their presence as just an isolated phenomenon of fallen human nature. They will repay the efforts of much study in Christian life for they undoubtedly play a part in the sad spectacle of the abandonment of religious practice. Indifference, among other reasons, certainly is one cause, but rejection and canalization of aggression against authority in this way are psychological entities which need careful examination in the future. The opportunity, of course, lies in offering the means by which these aggressive feelings can be integrated in the psyche without damaging it. Psychoanalysis offers the means of rendering the unconscious element conscious and therefore capable of insightful and rational management. Other forms of psychotherapy similarly are untangling the knots of, and bringing insight into the cause of, such feelings and helping the patient to handle them. Christianity, while fully cognizant of all these techniques and working through them, offers in addition a counsel of perfection which is older than all other methods of treatment: "Brethren, put ye on as the elect of God, holy and beloved, the bowels of mercy, benignity, humility, modesty, patience, bearing with one another and forgiving one another, if any have a complaint against another; even as the Lord has forgiven you, so do you also. But above all these things have charity which is the bond of perfection" (Col. 3. 12–13). Psychotherapy does indeed bring understanding, but in turn needs to learn that love is required to complete the process.

The experience of guilt feelings is of crucial interest both to psychiatry and religion. Guilt in the setting of the primordial myth is the consequence of the events that took place therein. And guilt in analytical theory is closely woven with frustrated and repressed sexual and aggressive desires. There is little doubt that this is experienced in these situations, but once again these instances do not exhaust man's capacity for guilt. If all other occasions are no more than disguised expressions of inhibition or discharge of libido and aggression, then any discussion becomes meaningless. In practice, this view cannot be substantiated, and the Christian again contradicts no unequivocal psychological tenet when he insists that, besides pathological guilt, there is far more commonly in every human being the natural reaction from behaviour which contravenes the sense of right and wrong. At times, a great deal of experience is required to dissect the pathological elements from normal responses and in neurotic patients there may be little left of the latter. In spite of this, no service is rendered to the patient by denying the existence of guilt consequent on wrong behaviour, for whatever the theoretical standpoint of the doctor, the patient knows and feels the need for expiation and reparation which, in the Catholic Church, finds its fulfilment in the sacrament of penance. Helping the neurotic patient to discriminate between morbid and normal sense of guilt can be a complex matter, needing much patience and considerable understanding of psychological principles. This is a subject on which research and information can be exchanged with considerable advantage between the disciplines of theology and psychiatry.

This can only begin when communication between the two subjects is conducted in meaningful language. When such common words as guilt, sexuality, aggression connote so many different concepts the likelihood of misunderstanding is considerable. The psychoanalytical terminology of super-ego, id, repression, suppression, defences, etc., can be extremely confusing and the Christian terms, conscience, grace, atonement, faith, the Church, etc., may have no meaning even for those who appreciate the necessity of having a greater knowledge of the Christian faith. There is an urgent need for well-informed experts to learn each other's language and, if possible, to simplify it in mutually recognizable terms. Integration, not separation, is the next necessary step.

Even when meaningful semantic coexistence is present there will still be room for differences of opinion between psychoanalytic theory and Christianity in the goal of therapy. One favourite psychoanalytical concept of mental health is the state in which one's potential capacities are fully realized. Sir Aubrey Lewis has retorted to this with the simple answer that we all have deplorable potentialities as well as desirable ones.[3] Christianity considers these deplorable potentialities the necessary consequence of original sin by means of which man has been deprived of his capacity for smooth, integrated and non-pathological activity and is saddled with the propensities of disease, psychological, physical and spiritual. Any system of psychiatry which totally ignores man's obligations and aspirations in the spiritual order cannot but diminish his stature and be incomplete.

This excessive preoccupation with psychoanalytical theory has unfortunately overshadowed other aspects of psychiatry which are intimately related to Christianity. Sociological research is becoming increasingly important in the total setting of etiological contributions to psychological disturbances. The social and environmental situation of any person has undoubted repercussions both in the development of personality and as sources for actively precipitating episodes of disorder. The Judaeo-Christian tradition has remained unequivocally clear in the importance it attaches to stable marriage, the integration of family units into a coherent community within which exist the facilities for interdependence and mutual help, motivated by common goals and ideals

[3] A. Lewis, "Health as a Social Concept", *British Journal of Sociology* (1953), IV, p. 2.

consistent with the physical, psychological and spiritual nature of man. Research into such subjects as suicide, the treatment of alcoholism, juvenile delinquency, adult crime and drug addiction have shown consistently that the disorders and outcome are closely linked with disturbances, minor and major, in the norms which Christianity emphasizes and upholds in the face of much contemporary opposition. Sadly, it has to be acknowledged that only too often the exchange between Christians and others in these matters becomes a matter of offering beliefs related to our faith and a painful surprise at their rejection when their apparent rationality does not commend them to others. When the obvious alternative of empirical observation and scientific formulation based on these beliefs is pursued, it is attacked on the basis that human behaviour is a domain ill-suited for such observation where intuitive subjective knowledge lies supreme. And so the tug of war proceeds relentlessly, Scientific Humanism seeking unattainable certainty, and Christianity unable to communicate its vital and important contributions through lack of acceptable channels. This is an unhappy situation needing urgent remedy on the lines that scientific means are tools which Christianity cannot ignore if its truths are to make the necessary impact on the present scene in psychiatry. Not all that is accepted by faith lends itself to such investigations but a good deal does and until we exchange opinions for facts we cannot expect as a right to take our proper place in the fields of psychology, psychiatry and sociology.

Throughout this book it has been emphasized that the unique contribution of Christianity to the subject is its ability to see in man, over and above his limitations and disturbances, the image of God and to apply the indefinable but unique contribution of love. No other branch of medicine creates such a vast need for this and none has received such a meagre contribution from the Christian community. We are living at a time in the history of mankind when a unique opportunity is being offered to make amends. It will be a great pity if we neglect it.

SELECT BIBLIOGRAPHY

In this series: BIOT, René: *What is Life?*; LE TROCQUER, René: *What is Man?*; MARSHALL, John: *Medicine and Morals*; TREVETT, Reginald F.: *The Church and Sex.*

BOUYER, Louis: *Woman and Man with God*, London, Darton, Longman and Todd, 1960.

CARRÉ, A. M., O.P.: *The Everlasting Priest*, London, Geoffrey Chapman, 1960.

DALBIEZ, Roland: *Psychoanalytical Method and the Doctrine of Freud*, two volumes, London and New York, Longmans, 1941.

FORD, J. C., S.J.: *Depth Psychology, Morality and Alcoholism*, Weston, Mass., Weston College Press, 1951.

FORDHAM, Frieda: *An Introduction to Jung's Psychology*, Harmondsworth and Baltimore, Penguin Books, 1953.

HAGMAIER, G., and GLEASON, R. W.: *Moral Problems Now*, London and New York, Sheed and Ward, 1960.

JELLINEK, E. M.: *The Disease Concept of Alcoholism*, New Haven, Conn., Hillhouse Press, 1960.

JONES, Ernest: *Life and Work of Sigmund Freud*, three volumes, London, Hogarth Press, and New York, McGraw-Hill, 1953, 1955, 1957.

KINSEY, A. C., and others: *Sexual Behaviour in the Human Female*, London and Philadelphia, Saunders, 1953; *Sexual Behaviour in the Human Male*, London and Philadelphia, Saunders, 1948.

MARSHALL, John: *The Ethics of Medical Practice*, London, Darton, Longman and Todd, 1960.

MAYER-GROSS, W., SLATER, E., and ROTH, M.: *Clinical Psychiatry*, London, Cassell, 1960, and Baltimore, Williams and Wilkins, 1955.

MESSENGER, Ernest C.: *Two in One Flesh*, three volumes, London, Sands, 1948, and Westminster, Md, Newman Press, 1955.

SCHNECK, J. M.: *A History of Psychiatry*, Springfield, Ill., C. C. Thomas, 1960.

STEVAS, N. St J.: *Life, Death and the Law*, London, Eyre and Spottiswoode, 1961.

VANDERVELDT, James H., and ODENWALD, P.: *Psychiatry and Catholicism*, New York and London, McGraw-Hill, 1957.

WEST, D. J.: *Homosexuality*, London, Duckworth, 1955.

WHITE, Victor, O.P.: *God and the Unconscious*, London, Harvill, and New York, Harper, 1952; *Soul and Psyche*, London, Harvill, and New York, Harper, 1960.

ZILBOORG, G., and HENRY, G. W.: *A History of Medical Psychology*, New York, Norton, 1941.

The Twentieth Century Encyclopedia of Catholicism

*The number of each volume indicates
its place in the over-all series
and not the order of publication.*

All titles are subject to change.